T0121902

JOYCE KING

HATE CRIME

A former reporter and anchor for a CBS radio affiliate, Joyce King is an award-winning twenty-year broadcast veteran. She also writes guest columns and opinion pieces for *USA Today, The Christian Science Monitor,* and *The Dallas Morning News.* This is her first book. She lives in Dallas.

HATE CRIME

JOYCE KING

HATE CRIME

The Story of a Dragging in Jasper, Texas

ANCHOR BOOKS

A Division of Random House, Inc.

New York

FIRST ANCHOR BOOKS EDITION, DECEMBER 2003

Copyright © 2002 by Joyce King

All rights reserved under International and Pan-American Copyright
Conventions. Published in the United States by Anchor Books, a division
of Random House, Inc., New York, and simultaneously in Canada by
Random House of Canada Limited, Toronto. Originally published in
hardcover in the United States by Pantheon Books, a division of
Random House, New York, in 2002.

Anchor Books and colophon are registered trademarks of
Random House, Inc.

Grateful acknowledgment is made to *The New York Times* for permission
to reprint excerpts from "In America: Staring at Hatred" by Bob Herbert
(2/28/1999). Copyright © 2001 by the New York Times Co.
Reprinted by permission of The New York Times.

The Library of Congress has cataloged the Pantheon edition as follows:
King, Joyce, 1959–
Hate crime : the story of a dragging in Jasper, Texas / Joyce King.
1. Byrd, James, d. 1998. 2. Murder—Texas—Jasper.
3. Hate crimes—Texas—Jasper.
4. African American men—Crimes against—
Texas—Jasper. 5. Racism—Texas—Jasper.
6. Jasper (Tex.)—Race relations. I. Title.
HV6534.J36.K56 2002
364.15'23'09764159—dc21
2001058074

Anchor ISBN: 978-0-385-72195-0

Author photograph © Constance Ashley
Book design by M. Kristen Bearse

www.anchorbooks.com

147468846

For Carlotta Monique Nation

1964–2001

The desire to turn away from a crime as grotesque as the murder of James Byrd, Jr. is understandable. Once justice is done, what is the point of wallowing in the hideousness of the crime? . . . There is a need to understand the rage and the impulses that lead so many to mayhem in the name of some warped sense of superiority. . . . Dragging someone to his death behind a truck may be unusual. But torturing, maiming and killing people because they fit a despised profile is an everyday occurrence. We can't stop it if we aren't even willing to look at it.

—BOB HERBERT, *The New York Times*

CONTENTS

HATE CRIME

PROLOGUE

As the sheriff of Jasper County daydreamed about an invigorating round of golf, he hummed down the highway to Dallas. Hitting the links on a gorgeous day was the anticipated payoff for the 250-mile trip Billy Rowles decided to make on a magnificent Sunday morning. But he would not putt one single time. An hour into his excursion, the veteran lawman overheard an urgent message on the two-way radio.

Rowles listened carefully to the panicked voices of his dispatchers and deputies. A black body had been found in the middle of Huff Creek Road, in a predominantly African-American community of the same name. Rowles found a place to turn around his truck, a white wide-body Ford F-250. He grabbed his mobile phone to check in with Alice Rector, one of the dispatchers. She confirmed that what the sheriff heard was indeed true.

Rowles didn't bother with red lights or sirens; traffic was predictably sparse. He floored the gas pedal, broke all the speed limits to get home. A short time later, Rowles was on the outskirts of the little town he loves. Huff Creek Road played cruel host to a steady stream of law enforcement officials. Residents poured out to examine the broken, naked black body. Nervous investigators, including the entire fourteen-deputy Sheriff's Department and most of Jasper's eighteen police officers, helped seal off the area to prevent contamination of crime scene evidence.

A frightened father, worried about a son who did not make it home Saturday night, moaned and wondered aloud if the black body was that of his son. A neighbor whose house was nearby studied the face and cautioned others that the devil was loose: "It doesn't matter who he catches." At least one officer at the scene, Sergeant James Carter, knew exactly who had been snared. It was another man's son.

The only African-American in the sheriff's department, Carter was a constant source of pride for thousands in the Piney Woods of East Texas. They trusted and respected him, a man whose rich mahogany features, chiseled honest face, and coal black hands offered comfort to many. They counted on the handsome deputy to make sure truth and justice prevailed for them. Like other investigators at the scene, Carter fielded questions from scared residents, then approached the disfigured body.

As he watched his white colleagues unroll yellow investigative tape, Carter knew in his heart it was James Byrd, Jr., a childhood friend. But a few of the other investigators were convinced it was someone who merely resembled Byrd. The quiet deputy, meanwhile, continued to interview and calm members of the community. Plainclothes and uniformed men bagged piece after piece of evidence, including keys and a wallet. More than twenty-five officers compared notes as they tracked a three-mile trail of dried blood and flesh. A driver's license easily ruled out the missing son and identified James Byrd, Jr. Determined to do everything by the book, officers waited for positive identification from fingerprints before alerting the family. While they waited, teams split up to check out possible leads. One came from inside the dead man's wallet—a simple grocery store receipt.

Carter made the short drive with other investigators to check out store surveillance tape, video that confirmed what he already knew. Verification was instant. James Byrd, Jr., walked out of the H.E.B. Pantry on Saturday night, June 6, 1998.

"It just did something to me as soon as I saw that walk," Carter sighed. Unmistakably, the strut belonged to a man the deputy grew up with, hung out and remained friends with, even though, as adults, they were sometimes on opposite sides of the law.

Back at the Aubrey E. Cole Law Enforcement Center, sheriff's headquarters on Burch Street, Carter took a call from his boss and informed Billy Rowles that the body had just been positively identified.

The man everyone in town knows as "Billy" slowly left the crime scene with a lump in his throat. Rowles drove, not that eager, not that fast, from Huff Creek Road to 101 Burch Street to pick up Carter.

Neither man—both out of uniform because it was a Sunday—wanted to make the three-minute trip to 128 West Broad Street. On the abbreviated ride, Sergeant Carter searched his mind for the right words and silently recalled how his boyhood friend stood in front of his house to "shoot the breeze" two weeks before his tragic death. Byrd prophetically assured Carter then that one day, as a singer, he would "put Jasper on the map." Carter couldn't help but think how he vowed, "Millions of people are going to know my name."

Once there, the two lawmen looked around the close-knit racially mixed neighborhood, just a few blocks from headquarters. Rowles and Carter—one white, one black, the sheriff in a ten-gallon hat and the loyal deputy in a department-issued baseball cap, both faces different shades of flush—parked directly in front of the Byrd family home. Paul Brister, the chief deputy, joined the grim procession, along with Dorie Coleman, a local mortician. They converged at the front steps at the speckled chestnut frame house.

Betty Boatner, a full-figured, attractive brown-skinned woman, was first to spot them. Boatner, home with her parents, looked gravely at the four men, inspected their pity-filled faces, and instantly started to cry. If Revelation 6:8 made sense to anyone, it did to her: *And I looked, behold a pale horse: and his name that sat on him was Death, and Hell followed with him.* "Here come the sheriff, James, and Mr. Coleman," Boatner cried as she informed her parents. As the group of men took slow-motion steps, Boatner was sure of one thing—whatever it was these men came to say on a Sunday afternoon was bad. The sight of county lawmen with their long faces and sad eyes accompanied by the polite man who buried the dead provided only one clue: The pale horse was being led home.

Intimations just hours before, including a news bulletin on television and radio about the black male victim of a hideous death, did not strike familiar. The thought that the dead man out on Huff Creek Road was the one they affectionately called "Son" never entered the minds of anyone in the Byrd household.

Seventy-three-year-old James Byrd, Sr., amazingly stronger than his years would suggest, had gotten up bright and early, as he always does on Sunday mornings. Just after seven, the small, dark, bespectacled deacon dutifully prepared for service at the Greater New Bethel Baptist Church on Martin Luther King Boulevard. Inside the vanilla-brick sanctuary, everything was not praise as usual.

Rev. Kenneth Lyons, studious minister at Greater New Bethel, rose from his thronelike chair, paused, and gave a serious glance to the few African-American men in his congregation. Lyons had looked out at the distressed masculine faces, while faithful sisters still remained in various women-only classes. Finally, the minister uttered a stern warning: "Be cautious as you move about. Be careful."

Black men of all shapes, sizes, ages, and skin tones gazed around the room at each other for comfort, for support. With an eerie look and a sound frighteningly reminiscent of Civil Rights days, Rev. Lyons lowered his voice to explain to the small attentive crowd that a black man had been found savagely murdered. Lyons offered another gory detail—the gruesome discovery of the unidentified man, found beheaded, "is extra cause for concern in our community."

Brother Byrd, like most chilled by the offensive news, understood the ripple of fragmented fear and anger, but had no particular reason to believe the dead man was his son, his namesake. The older Byrd shook his head at the sorry state of affairs and clung tightly to his Bible, with a deep sorrow for some poor family.

Sunday school dismissed, James Byrd, Sr., prepared for the worship service. Perched on his favorite pew, a thick, comfortable green cushion with matching carpet the color of money, at a heavenly little church in which he felt protected and loved, the God-fearing deacon began to pray. After the service, he continued his routine and headed home to spend a peaceful Sunday afternoon with his wife.

Six steps led to a curved stretch of sidewalk, connected to a front porch of winding greenery. A wooden rail offered the sheriff, deputies, and mortician little support for what was ahead. Painted a fudge color on the sides, the neat house had three lighter shades of brown in front—a kaleidoscopic overlay of vertical rows in tan, milk-chocolate, and the color of tree bark.

A weatherized screen door opened about the same time Rowles and Carter neared the edge of the small front porch. Signs of life were everywhere: Elephant-ear plants stood at attention, while other leafy vines blended in. A single red rose bush to the left of the door, out in the yard, was almost hidden underneath a sticker bush. Smells of a down-home Sunday dinner wafted through the small garden.

The veteran lawmen had delayed delivering the news for as long as they could. With as much compassion as possible, the sheriff of Jasper County told Stella and James Byrd, Sr., "A man found dead on Huff Creek Road this morning has been positively identified as your son, James Byrd, Jr."

Rowles thought of the excruciatingly painful words he was not about to say—that forty-nine-year-old James Byrd, Jr., their son, their brother, their loved one, was out in the middle of the road like so many scattered pieces of a puzzle, dragged to death like an animal. He could not say that.

They heard the ungodly news three times before it made a dent. They were stunned and incredulous at first, then angry and unassailably sad. Words of comfort, unanswered questions, and a plethora of emotions merged into an ocean of sorrow. Betty Boatner tried to comfort her aging parents as all three bravely mustered up the strength to continue listening. The pale horse was gone, mission completed. Nothing for the Byrd family would ever be the same. They knew this. "Son" was gone forever. In his place—body parts scattered over Huff Creek Road, changed and rearranged. All that was left of a loved one were personal effects strewn all over a nameless logging road.

Betty Boatner immediately began to call family members, including her six other siblings, to tell them the unthinkable news—not only had Son been murdered, but for some reason unbeknown to the family he was the victim of an atrocious deed, done under the cover of darkness. The ghastly nightmare they starred in woke a sleeping nation.

Overwhelmed, the Byrd family watched the sun set. It brought a glimmer of comfort that their tiny home was filled with friends and neighbors ready to take the next difficult step with them. Night fell quickly. Someone remembered it was still Sunday. They prayed for justice and embraced Ecclesiastes 3: 1–2: *To every thing there is a season, and a time to every purpose under the heaven. A time to be born, and a time to die.* For James Byrd, Jr., the circle was complete.

Part One

BLACK AND WHITE COLLISION

ONE

Jasper is extremely small, a typical East Texas bedroom community. Home to nearly 8,000 people, it is the county seat, a proud distinction for any Texas town. Ask some residents and they'll tell you the city of Jasper is historically as well as geographically too near the likes of Vidor, Texas, a defiant Klan stronghold about fifty-five miles away. Folks who don't belong in Vidor, particularly black folks, steer clear of it. Listen to a few others and Jasper is a bastion of racial equality, a prosperous and fair place to raise kids, to set a good example.

Enlightened people who live within Jasper's city limits point to its obvious differences—their mayor, R. C. Horn, is black; prominent leaders of both races get along and work well together; and the census shows that the town itself is roughly made up of equal parts: Though it fluctuates, Jasper is approximately 45 percent African-American and about 48 percent Anglo, with most of the remaining percentage Hispanic.

It is a pretty place, strikingly clean, contemporary, but still connected to timeless traditions. Jasper has a rich history and attracts annual tourists for hugely profitable bass-fishing tournaments. A sprinkling of brand-name chain hotels, as well as quaint little lodging houses, lots of churches, tasty homemade food, and friendly people give Jasper a reputation for being a cut above most East Texas towns. It even has what proud residents jokingly call "the Mall," its huge twenty-four-hour Wal-Mart Supercenter, the biggest deal in town.

That the slow pace in Jasper does not hold much interest for its young people is something with which town leaders constantly struggle. There are five schools in the Jasper Independent School District, only one of them a high school. Teens who graduate from the high school usually head for higher academic ground or better-paying jobs at plants in larger Texas cities, like Beaumont or Port Arthur. A few others make the short commute to the southern end of the county to work at plants like the large paper mill in Evadale. Others make a decent living at oil refineries, mostly next door in Louisiana. Those who stay behind don't have many options, unless a relative owns a lumber mill. A lot of the other jobs pay only the minimum wage, or slightly better.

Routines reserved for weekdays—school, church events, and work—take place in a highly public fashion, in the open for all to participate in and judge. For the majority, the medium gait of life in Jasper is perfect—not too fast, not too slow. Residents take care of business and look out for each other. They do so without all the big-city hassles, without the rush and crush of traffic nightmares and rude citified behavior. Come six o'clock Friday night, things slow to a crawl; local streets empty as people rest and change their body clocks to reflect weekend time. By Saturday, many make the seventy-mile trek to Beaumont or twice that distance to faraway Houston, to break the monotony of Bud long necks, plate-sized chicken-fried steaks, and two- and three-star movies at the Twin Cinema. Given that there is little to do in Jasper on the weekend, others routinely grab Burger King specials or pack up their own food for picnic get-togethers at nearby Martin Dies Jr. State Park. Dozens more hitch up the boat or Jet Skis and head for Steinhagen Lake, Toledo Bend, or Sam Rayburn Reservoir, a beautiful body of water named after the native son who proudly served as one of the nation's most colorful Speakers of the House of Representatives and who is widely remembered for his dogged insistence that his colleagues vote for the Civil Rights Act of 1964. Others, shunning big-city lights and nearby tourist attractions, love the quiet serenity and beauty of Jasper.

Like any small town, Jasper has its share of hotheads and lawbreakers, but for the most part, decent citizens want good, clean fun. Without any large nightclubs, a favorite Jasper pastime is an old-fashioned, blue-light house party with good music and close friends. Attendees can drink as much as they want in the privacy of someone's home and avoid the weekend crackdown on public alcohol consumption. Texas peace officers are rare but firm upholders of the state's hard-to-enforce open-container law: Don't get caught driving while taking a swig. Residents make sure, day or night, that whatever they are drinking behind the wheel in a brown paper bag is a Coke or cream soda.

Yet, liquor is plentiful on the outskirts of Jasper, a dry community located within a very wet county of more than 30,000 people. Many don't think it's a problem to serve alcohol at a private, invitation-only house party, even if they do live in a dry town. Some residents have even been known to bootleg—make their own barrel whiskey—an illegal activity that does not sit well with law-abiding neighbors. Jasper's pristine location in the Deep South Bible Belt provokes more than a few upright Christians to morally chastise their neighbors. One anonymous citizen posed the provocative question "If Jasper's really a dry town and folks can't buy liquor here, why are there so many alcoholics?"

On Saturday night, June 6, 1998, Jimmie Mays had the perfect reason to have one of those old-fashioned parties at his house. Besides his son's birthday, it was his twentieth wedding anniversary. James

Byrd, Jr., a forty-nine-year-old unemployed former vacuum sales-man, was among the guests who showed up at the large gray and white trailer home. Byrd was popular in Jasper, well known for his charisma and beautiful singing voice. In and out of minor legal scrapes since high school, Byrd was often described by family and friends as a man who never hurt anyone but himself. The divorced father of three was proud of his deserved reputation as a lover of life but equally ashamed of a very real drinking problem that sometimes left him lonely and alone.

Besides Byrd, more than forty people turned out to eat good food, drink good whiskey, sing, dance, and play cards and domi-noes. At the end of a long week, many in the crowd were simply glad to be among friends and grateful that someone was in the mood to host a Saturday night house party. George "Billy" Mahathay was right in the thick of things.

Handsome, unmistakably a ladies' man, with curly jet-black hair and almond-colored eyes, Mahathay was something of a local fixture around town. The burly, friendly-looking owner of Billy's BBQ couldn't help but notice a slight difference in his boyhood friend. "Byrd's not his usual self," Mahathay would later testify, "quiet, not singing and dancing like he normally does."

Everyone at the lively get-together laughed, talked, drank, and toasted Mays and his wife. The weather was a tad warm, but pleas-antly bearable. By tough Texas standards, the Mays' house party was a great success, a savory musical gumbo of blues, soul, hip-hop, jazz—a little something for everyone. Byrd half-enjoyed the music and wrestled with distant thoughts, maybe a personal dilemma. He seemed distracted but continued to drink and joke around. For whatever reason, Byrd did not belt out the tunes he was famous for.

Like a few others, Mahathay had had a bit too much to drink, but it was Saturday night and he was among friends. As the festive anniversary party came to a close, he chose a more sober friend, Samuel Williams, to give him a ride home. He smiled at the host and bid the Mays family goodnight.

The neat trailer emptied as the party ended. Williams and Mahathay left sometime between 1:30 and 1:45 A.M. on Sunday, June 7. It wasn't too far to Mahathay's house, almost around the corner from Jimmie Mays, but Mahathay was glad for the ride.

Right near Martin Luther King Boulevard, the tipsy passenger noticed James Byrd, Jr., on Bowie Street, near Mahathay's house. The men did not stop to give Byrd a ride; they believed he could make it on his own, as he had so many times before. Though Byrd owned an old car, one that had been out of commission a whole month, anyone who knew Byrd also knew that he was not afraid to walk anywhere in town. It was not uncommon for black people to walk in Jasper. Or white people, for that matter. Public transportation was almost nonexistent and there was no bus line or major taxi service. People paid small sums, if they had it, for neighbors and relatives to give them rides to necessary places. Or, they just walked.

When Billy Mahathay entered his residence, he was so sure Byrd could make it home that he never looked back. Byrd zigzagged down the road in a drunken stupor, taking step after wide step, a route he almost knew blindfolded, one that usually got him home in pitch-black darkness.

At about the same time the fun ended at the Mays home, a private party also wrapped up across town at the Timbers Apartments, upstairs in number 214, a tiny rented space on West Gibson Street, the main drag in Jasper.

Twenty-one-year-old Keisha Adkins was there, along with her former boyfriend, twenty-three-year-old John William King, a handsome local with brown hair and brown eyes, and a justified reputation as the hotheaded boy next door who can turn abruptly nasty.

Earlier in the evening, Adkins had run into King at the local Wal-Mart. Out of jail only a few months, the persuasive talker extended an invitation to his apartment. Flattered by renewed attention from King, Adkins examined his 5-foot-8-inch frame and saw that King had put on a little weight. Still, he looked good to Adkins as she mulled over the tempting proposition.

At about 10:30 P.M., shy, soft-spoken Keisha Adkins, a pale brunette, firmly knocked on King's door. The Timbers was a plain apartment complex; the wood-planked stairs and a small landing were barely large enough for two people.

Adkins discovered that King was not alone. Jailhouse buddy Lawrence Russell Brewer, a thirty-one-year-old convict from Sulphur Springs, Texas, had arrived in town only days before and was staying with King. Adkins knew Brewer was new to Jasper, and she looked him over and noted his physical attributes: He was small in stature, about 5 feet 6, 145 pounds, dark hair, and beady eyes. Remarkably muscular, he was a tough little man who looked as if he could take care of himself.

King and Brewer, a mutual admiration society of misfits, celebrated their victorious reunion, free men, at the same time, out in the world together. They started to drink cold Bud Lights and Coors Lights way before Adkins arrived. King playfully took off his shirt, another Saturday night ritual in June that in some neighborhoods went hand in hand with beer, white boys, and the pursuit of babes.

Not easily intimidated, Adkins studied King's drastically changed body—slightly potbellied and riddled with menacing tattoos. Adkins would later testify they did not offend her. The silly depiction of cartoon character Woody Woodpecker wearing a Klan robe was mildly humorous—if a person liked racist jokes. King's other tattoos were not so comical. One in particular, of a hanging black man, was neither a joke nor a cartoon. King did not openly discuss his radical views on race with Adkins, nor did he hide them. Tattooed arms, back, and torso spoke volumes. There was even a drawing of the Disney character Tinkerbell, located on King's genitals. It was the one tattoo King was ready to show Adkins privately.

While the ex-lovers renewed their relationship in the master bedroom, Brewer kept busy with loud music and the phone. He was on the lookout for King's current girlfriend. Brewer couldn't be happy that his role was relegated to watchdog, but that did not stop him from consuming more beer—beer the two convicted burglars had stolen earlier. Without money, there was not much else to do in Jasper on a Saturday night.

Kylie Greeney, King's very pregnant girlfriend, showed up at the front door. She banged on the door and forcefully demanded to be let in. While Adkins and King were together, just a few feet away, Brewer was left with strict orders not to let in the future mother of King's child. More afraid of King than of his girlfriend, Brewer faithfully guarded the front door. Upset and frustrated, Greeney finally gave up and stomped back down the steps and out of the complex.

Sometime after midnight, King's twenty-three-year-old roommate, Shawn Allen Berry, showed up. Berry, the only one of the three friends who held a regular job, had finished up work as manager of the Twin Cinema, locked the movie theater for the night, and returned to the one-bedroom apartment.

Highly regarded as someone who could hold his own in a fight, Berry always carried a sharp, straight blade. Though he was the shortest of the three friends—just 5 feet 5, 160 pounds—Berry earned respect as a scrappy young man, one with dependable transportation, good looks, and a well-documented adventurous spirit. He was more personable than King or Brewer, and had adequate social skills and a number of hobbies, including bull riding. Berry lived for the end of each hard week. He couldn't wait to grab a cold beer to let off a little Saturday night steam. As usual, Shawn Berry was ready to roll.

Before June 6, King and Adkins had talked only by phone; they were excited to see one another. Oblivious to the painfully small apartment and extra companions, any potential discomfort or embarrassment wasn't apparent when they emerged from King's bedroom. Adkins hadn't seen her old boyfriend in two long years.

King walked Adkins to her car. His impatient running buddies, eager to leave, brainstormed ideas on how to spend Saturday night in Jasper. Brewer wanted to try and find a girl who had earlier invited them to a party, where they might meet more girls. Berry, whose vehicle they rode around in, was restless, ready to go with the flow. But all did not go according to plan. Adkins was the only female the trio would get to see that Saturday night. Unfortunately for them, her presence at the Timbers Apartments helped to establish a crucial time line.

When all four walked out of King's apartment and concluded the quarantined party, Adkins believed the time was about 1:45 A.M., give or take a few minutes, on Sunday. Adkins got into her car, saw the three men climb into Berry's ashy-gray step-side pickup. She later testified as to the seat assignments, "Shawn is driving, Russell sits in the middle and Bill is on the right side."

The three men drove away, and for a few minutes traveled just ahead of Adkins' car. She watched three animated heads bob and turn, fingers point and gesture. After Adkins turned off toward her home, forty-five miles away in Fred, the three partygoers loudly continued on down the road. Keisha Adkins rushed to get home before Brian, her common-law husband, pulled up from his grave-yard shift.

Just as the three white boys drove off looking for entertainment in one part of Jasper, James Byrd, Jr., left Jimmie Mays' anniversary party on the other side of town, in the black community. Four lives were set to collide.

James Byrd, Jr., continued to stagger down Martin Luther King. He was drunk, but in the back of his mind, he believed he could make it to one of two places—his tiny, subsidized apartment on Pollard Street or his parents' home on nearby West Broad. Hopeful, but disoriented, he stumbled on.

Byrd, a lifelong resident, was easily recognized by many. People often spoke to him. Authorities picked him up. Total strangers liked to hear him sing. Although he took some wrong turns in life, Byrd was obsessed by a dream of fame and fortune with a new career that would allow him to perform.

Eighteen-year-old Steven Scott instantly identified Byrd on the side of the road, even slowed down. The lanky, well-mannered col-lege student thought to offer Byrd a ride home, nearly did, but quickly changed his mind and followed "his conscience," which told him to drive on and leave Byrd alone. To the young man, it wasn't worth the trouble because Byrd appeared "very drunk," meandering all over the road. Momentarily remorseful, Scott drove right on by Byrd; he was the second acquaintance or friend to do so. After all, a lot of people in Jasper walked to get where they were going.

Scott was on his way home from a popular Beaumont nightclub. Determined to beat his mother's curfew, if only by a few minutes, and maybe get some rest before Sunday church service, Scott drove on. He did not want to use the few precious minutes he had left to "fool with Mr. Byrd." Scott's unshakable time line tallied with what Adkins later told authorities. She placed King, Brewer, and Berry in the pickup shortly before 2 A.M. A few minutes later, Scott saw a fourth passenger in the truck, noting with surprise that Byrd was "riding on the back of a step-side truck," which zoomed right by him with three shadowy figures in the cab. His mother's front porch, right near a bright streetlight on Bowie, gave Scott a pretty decent view, "I saw three people inside the truck"—he was adamant—"and Mr. Byrd on the back."

The hyped-up friends rode around the whole of Jasper, a repetitious little adventure that only took a few minutes. They searched for the home of some girl who wanted them to drop by her party, but couldn't find it because Brewer had bungled or forgotten all the directions. King and Berry got mad. They were eager to chase blondes, brunettes, or redheads. It would not matter because the threesome didn't have any luck in the all but empty streets. Most folks were either headed home or already there.

A red and white cooler, which contained beer, rested in the back of Berry's rickety 1982 Ford. They drank and rode. When they couldn't find any women, somebody got the idea that it might be fun to tie a chain around a wooden mailbox, uproot it, and drag it down the street. It was fun, for a while, but once the mailbox excitement played out and the beer in the cooler started to run low, they decided to take their fun to another level.

Moments later, the pranksters discovered a black man walking in the road, minding his own business. Their next diversion was about to begin. The unwitting victim believed someone would finally help him find the way home.

"Hey, you need a ride?" Berry called to Byrd, a man he knew by sight but not by name. No response. Berry tried again: "Do you want to go home or what?" Byrd was not so drunk he didn't recognize at least one friendly face, the one behind the wheel. "No, I'll hang out with you white boys for a while," he responded. Byrd, who served time for theft, and Berry had the same parole officer; their paths may have crossed before. James Byrd, Jr., slowly climbed on the back of Shawn Berry's truck. He had no reason to fear. After all, everybody in Jasper knew everybody else.

Byrd quickly positioned himself farther up the truck's hard metal floor, back-to-back with King, Brewer, and Berry, who were all inside. The truck didn't have its tailgate on, so it was dangerous to sit too near the rear. An offer of beer was made and Byrd did not hesitate. The square picnic cooler was right near Byrd; he reached in, popped a top, and started to drink. Byrd was dog-tired and thirsty from a circular walk that had gotten him no closer to home.

The hospitality ended before Byrd could even consume the whole can of beer. Berry's simple offer to give a black man a ride home set King off. Livid, he turned to Berry, red-faced and suddenly more sober than drunk, and made an announcement: "That's some ho-ass shit, picking up a fucking nigger." Apparently unfazed by the tone or by the kind of racist language he heard all the time, Berry drove on, laughed it off, wound all the way down

Martin Luther King Boulevard, picked up FM 776, a farm-to-market road, then turned on State Highway 63 and traveled east. A short time later, they pulled over at BJ's Grocery, a small mom-and-pop convenience store just off the highway. Though closed, it was at BJ's that the events quickly escalated to the beginning of the end for James Byrd, Jr. After the men relieved themselves out in the open, Byrd traded places with two men he did not know. Two avowed, die-hard racists, King and Brewer, posing as good color-blind Boy Scouts, volunteered their prime seats in the cab so a black man could sit up front.

Byrd, trusting and still inebriated, got in the cab with Berry while King and Brewer took their self-designated places, riding shotgun on the back of the truck, the fresh night air in their faces.

Byrd was mostly quiet. Still behind the wheel, Berry offered Byrd a smoke and headed for the off-road joy ride that King suggested earlier. Deep into the Texas thicket was an old logging road, a trail few could find by light of sun or moon. Suddenly, Berry made a wild turn from the main road. Byrd's full attention was, at last, aroused. "Where we going?" he asked. Berry answered, "We're just riding."

Byrd almost instantly found himself in darker, thicker woods. Berry's truck bounced up and down, glided in and out of giant dirt pockets on the unmarked, out-of-the-way logging road, until, without warning, King banged hard on top of the truck and yelled to Berry, "Stop for a minute."

Berry obeyed, but before he could turn off the engine, King and Brewer excitedly jumped from the side and rear of the truck. The loud motor raced on as King and Brewer violently pulled at Byrd to tear him from the truck.

Byrd, disabled, a chronic arthritis sufferer, about 5 feet 9 and 160 pounds, was trapped and suddenly in the battle of his life. He fought hard. For a tired, intoxicated man almost twice the age of his attackers, Byrd's defense was impressive. He kicked, screamed, hung on to the frame of the truck, yelled for help, all the while praying to figure out what he was up against. Not in complete control of his faculties, Byrd's motor skills were dull and awkward, but fear fueled a passionate self-defense. He fought harder.

According to later testimony, Berry bolted from the truck, ran to the other side, and made some halfhearted attempt to stop the attack. King and Brewer continued the difficult task at hand—prying Byrd out of the truck in order to "scare the shit" out of him. The struggle intensified, got louder, faster, more furious. No one could believe all the energy it took to peel Byrd's hands from the frame of the pickup. He hung on for dear life. No one heard his pleas for help. Agitated by Byrd's raw audacity to fight, King stepped back and shouted, "Fuck it, let's kill this nigger."

The assailants finally managed to rip Byrd from the truck's cab. Once they did, it was relatively easy to pull him to the ground. While Byrd still asked God for help, begging for mercy, they began to beat and kick him as hard as possible. The earth absorbed missed blows, swallowed up evidence. Berry wet his pants. His waste trickled down designer blue jeans and past his polo boots, to the same ground where fresh drops of blood had fallen. A cheap Zippo cigarette lighter with the word "Possum" and "KKK" engraved on it flew out of its owner's pocket. A brand-new souvenir baseball cap with SAN FRANCISCO emblazoned across the front was long gone from the victim's head. It was on the ground, joined by long-neck beer bottles, a partially empty pack of Marlboro Reds, cigarette butts, and a nut wrench with "Berry" scratched onto it. Pieces of a puzzle carelessly discarded, easy evidence for the state's prosecution.

Byrd was savagely beaten and kicked, maliciously hit about the body and head, too many blows to count. Brewer grabbed a can of black spray paint from the truck. Byrd still moved way too much. Brewer later admitted to pointing it right in Byrd's bruised face and spraying the black man with the black paint. King shouted, "Don't do that! Don't spray nobody in the face!" but Brewer asserted it was extra punishment and further humiliation for Byrd because he was mad that he hurt his foot kicking Byrd.

Seriously injured and unable to see, Byrd was stunned and helpless, flailing at anything he felt come near. Then, the hardest, hottest kick of all, straight to Byrd's head. He finally stopped fighting and dropped. He did not move again. He was blinded by the spray paint, flat on his back, out of breath, but still alive. His determined captors grabbed another item from the bed of the gray pickup—a used, rusty log chain.

Byrd's pants and underwear were pulled down to his ankles. Before they snatched loose his clothing, exposing Byrd in the most cruel physical way, King took a moment to explain to the others that the same thing was done in the old days to "niggers who messed with white women."

The log chain was unfolded and quickly looped around the ball on the hitch of the pickup, with each end strategically wrapped around Byrd's ankles. All three men jumped back into the truck's cab, prepared to drag a man while he was still alive. Though it was not too late to turn back, to stop, to call it off, not one of them did.

Before Byrd could reach his final destination, there was untold suffering, unimaginable pain. He felt every single weed, every endless speck of grass and dirt, every chasm, and every inch of asphalt.

The dragging started on the hemmed-in logging road. Not long after, Byrd's body slipped loose from the chain. They slammed on the brakes to recover their defenseless victim. Drunk with enthusiasm and frenzy, the driver backed up too far, too fast, possibly running over Byrd's extensively disfigured body, scraped, scratched, skinned alive. The body got tangled underneath the truck. Laughs echoed in the night, the driver accelerated forward, over Byrd once more. Someone jumped out. Seconds later, Byrd was rechained and the dragging resumed.

Partly conscious, Byrd used his elbows and knees to try to keep his head up off the road. Meanwhile, from inside the cab of the truck, yells of fun pierced the night. "Look, that nigger's bouncing all over the place." Laughter reverberated as Byrd's body was dragged through rocks, loamy dirt, tree branches, and trash. The truck turned left onto an adjoining blacktop artery, Huff Creek Road, up out of the heavy bush, off of the no-name logging road, out into a more open space where people lived, went to church, and buried their dead. Byrd was alive but could not scream.

With what little strength he had left, Byrd made a valiant effort to keep his head above the hard concrete. The truck's driver sped on, driving his brand of racism and hatred smack dab into the middle of a black community, bold as you please.

Byrd's naked body was hurled from one side of the road to the other, then he hit a culvert that decapitated him. His brutal tormentors continued to drag Byrd's headless body. Parts were torn from his body like twigs from a branch. They fell by the side of the road, in a ditch, then near a decrepit wood-frame building, and all along the road. His head, partially attached to a separated shoulder, was about a mile from the ripped lower torso. The once human face had drag marks on it.

What was left of his body was released from the chain near a small black cemetery, holy ground where speechless ancestors witnessed the deed. His dismembered body sent a message to all: You could be next!

Daybreak was near. Sunday morning filled the area with parishioners who normally attended Rose Bloom Baptist Church, an ordinary, sweetly innocent country house of worship. Death's path of three miles was there for all to see. People, mostly black people, had to walk this way. They lived here, loved and died here, and had witnessed this kind of hatred before. To yet another generation, it seemed a revival of the activities of the White Citizens' Council, a Civil Rights era committee of hood-free racists whose predecessors were brutal night riders with a preference for ropes and horses.

TWO

Investigators used bright red spray paint to circle places at the crime scene where three miles' worth of evidence had been discovered. More than seventy circles would be marked to identify Byrd's remains alone—bone, flesh, blood—pieces of a life. It was Sunday morning and the conscience of a small Southern county was about to undergo an unprecedented metamorphosis.

Only hours before, the criminals threw the almost 25-foot-long chain into the back of Berry's truck and headed home. Few comments were made during the short ride, but there was one important question: Shawn Berry wanted to know why they did it. A shallow response from King revealed nothing, produced a sobering silence.

Back at the apartment, talk of an alibi rattled their nerves and permeated their attempt at sleep. King insisted that Keisha Adkins would willingly provide the necessary alibi. Brewer didn't argue. Instead, he looked in vain for some smokes. Brewer hobbled on his good foot, headed straight for the truck. But the Marlboro Reds had disappeared. Brewer touched the hefty chain to see if any stray cigarettes were entwined in the metal or lodged between the chain and the truck's rusty bed.

Sometime after 5 A.M., King talked with Adkins on the phone. According to later testimony, she believed King was in a "normal mood" except for the urgent immediacy of wanting to see her again.

Berry tossed in a restless half-slumber on the couch. He couldn't help but think, over and over, how he should've gone straight to the police. Surely they would believe he had nothing to do with such a terrible crime. Berry's pro and con arguments were drowned out by an earlier thesis delivered by King: "Being there makes you just as guilty."

There was one person Berry thought to call for help. His uncle, Raymond Hopson, was a respected state trooper. Hopson would know what to do. Berry could tell him what happened, where to find the black man's body, and persuade Hopson that he had nothing to do with it. Berry didn't phone him right away; he needed more time to think.

The threesome tried hard to relax, settle down a little, but the question of why this crime was committed wouldn't go away. King's answer, "We're starting *The Turner Diaries* early," did not begin to explain it. Brewer mumbled something about how much his foot—the one he used to kick James Byrd, Jr., in the head—hurt. Meanwhile, King smugly told Berry, "Don't worry about it, bro."

All three continued to let the buzz of beer wear off and reality set in as they attempted to gain repose after a morning of murder in the woods.

Like any movie theater after a Saturday night crowd, Jasper's Twin Cinema needed cleaning up. The feature, *City of Angels*, had a pretty good turnout, including manager Shawn Berry, his girl-friend, Christie Marcontell, their baby son, Montana, and King's girlfriend, Kylie Greeney.

After he managed to get a few hours of sleep, Berry was ready to prepare the Twin Cinema for its first Sunday matinee. Sometimes

Brewer rode along to give Berry a hand. He was always promised money, but usually only got a pack of cigarettes. Not such a willing volunteer anymore, Brewer nonetheless went along that Sunday. King stayed behind.

Upstairs, just over the theater, was a private room with a few amenities, including a stash of cold beer and a bed. Berry had had enough to drink and didn't bother to see if the small bed would inspire any better brand of sleep than King's couch. Slightly calmer, Brewer made do with a fresh supply of cigarettes.

Wired, with a disheveled appearance, Berry had on the same clothes from Saturday night: Ralph Lauren jeans, polo boots, and a long-sleeve denim shirt. He had a lot on his mind. It never occurred to him to shower and change, even though his jeans had the faint scent of dried urine.

As they straightened up the theater, picking up empty popcorn boxes and moisture-beaded cups, there was little conversation between the two. Berry's mind replayed the horrific scene from a few hours earlier. It was like something out of a horror movie. His response—or lack of one—was trapped in turmoil between lips and larynx. Berry decided to make the call to his Uncle Raymond, a veteran trooper in the Department of Public Safety (DPS).

Berry desperately wanted to tell him what happened, how it all started, and to explain the fear that paralyzed him on Huff Creek Road. Instead, he lost his nerve and feigned morbid curiosity in the anonymous victim that everyone in the county was talking about over Sunday brunch. Hopson, puzzled at Berry's interest, answered his odd questions with the few sketchy details available.

The brief conversation ended before Berry could fill in the blanks or ask for advice. King and his girlfriend arrived at the theater, waiting for Brewer to finish so they could leave together. Berry missed an opportunity to distance himself from two men who were already plotting out the rest of a leisurely Sunday afternoon.

Instead of a dignified surrender to a trusted family member who might've walked him into the Jasper County Jail and encouraged him to aid authorities, Berry simply opted for a visit to a nearby car wash. It was time to get rid of incriminating evidence.

Tools, beer bottles, and sanding blocks were all removed from the back of the truck. Most of the frame looked as if it was scrubbed ghost-white, or had a grimy film left by too many bad wax jobs. After the log chain was unraveled and laid flat on the ground, powerful blasts of water were jet-sprayed by the wand to wash off any sand, prints, or blood.

Once the items were returned to the truck, a coin or two started the car-wash vacuum cleaner. As Berry thought of ways to avoid prison, the machine sucked up dirt, fibers, and any other evidence unseen by the naked eye.

Christie Marcontell phoned the apartment to speak with Berry, who had told her he intended to go straight home to bed after work on Saturday night. She was not exactly thrilled to discover it didn't happen that way. At one-thirty Sunday afternoon, King told Marcontell that her boyfriend was still asleep. She wondered if Berry would deliberately avoid her call, if he was upset that another man had bought her lunch the day before. Marcontell had no idea that Berry was hardly in the mood for a domestic squabble. Two hours later, she was at the movie theater with Berry and Brewer. Something was very wrong.

Marcontell instantly noticed that Berry was agitated, though he didn't appear to be jealous. She was sure there was something different about her man, but didn't link his mood to the shocking news that he and Brewer shared with her about a body being found on Huff Creek Road. The Sunday drama lent an air of citified mystery to an otherwise quiet country day. As there are few murders in Jasper County, Marcontell was intrigued but never connected the sensational crime to the young man she hoped to marry.

Rumors poured like bootleg whiskey in the prohibitionist county seat. Townspeople wanted to believe the deed was done elsewhere and the body dumped in their community. Since the murder occurred right near the Newton-Jasper county line, it was easier to believe that nothing so evil could come from their own. Some blamed a revitalized Klan element. Others argued it would be hard to resuscitate something that had never died. Klan or not, law enforcement officials carefully scrutinized similar departmental theories.

To avoid any suggestion of a compromised investigation, Sheriff Billy Rowles refused to allow anyone the chance to cite integrity issues concerning the collection and preservation of evidence. He had no doubt his county department, teamed up with the Jasper City Police, could do the job. Routinely paired for big cases, Rowles' gut instinct told him this case would require more backup than local police could provide. Together, they would need some assistance from the United States government. The sheriff informed the Federal Bureau of Investigation in Beaumont that Jasper needed help with a possible "hate crime." A few inner-circle critics disagreed with Rowles and weren't too happy he called in the feds. But Rowles, like several other key players, knew all too well how East Texas would be stereotyped by the national media. Even longtime Police Chief Harlan Alexander had to agree it was a tough case for just one department to handle. "You're not going to be smarter than all of us when we put our heads together," he told a group of reporters.

With so many white lawmen roaming the Huff Creek neighborhood for clues and witnesses, word about the murder began to spread across the state like an out-of-control prairie fire. Investigators warned the grieving family not to share specifics with anyone, especially the media. Mindful that no arrests had been made, they did not want anything, or anyone, to interfere with the capture of those responsible.

While Stella and James Byrd, Sr., tried to locate their other grown children and get them home as quickly as possible for a family meeting, investigators also prepared for a series of meetings to conduct extensive discussions about what the evidence suggested. Residents were asked to come forward with any information, any details on the whereabouts of the man identified as James Byrd, Jr. Lead investigators already knew his family last saw Byrd when he left a niece's bridal shower Saturday evening around 6 P.M.

Not far away at the Twin Cinema, Louis Berry joined Christie Marcontell to catch up with his younger brother. Louis was still angry with King from the night before. He and another friend, Tommy Faulk, liked to get together and play jam sessions with a black man nicknamed Gracie. Faulk played guitar and Berry played drums, while Gracie plucked bass. When King unknowingly approached a Saturday night party being thrown for Faulk, he did not know that Gracie, the host, was black. When King found out, he belligerently refused to enter the black man's home: "If you want to stay and fuck around with that nigger, fine." Louis Berry was infuriated at the insult to such a close friend. But with King and Brewer back at the Twin Cinema hanging out with his brother, he decided it was a waste of time to hold a grudge. Especially since they had so many common friends among their clique. Some of those same running buddies agreed to meet later for a casual game of volleyball to pass the time.

Sixteen-year-old Heather Hough was a popular girl who lived about ten miles outside Jasper in an even smaller town called Roganville. Hough first met King at the Twin Cinema, and they dated four or five times. Introduced by Berry, she and King were no longer romantically involved, but remained friends. She had only recently met his prison pal Brewer.

After sides were chosen, the friendly teams squared off to play volleyball. But not everyone was eager to join in. King bowed out of the game because of a sore injured arm. Brewer had on sandals, and the big toe on his right foot looked awful. He turned to Hough. "Do you mind playing volleyball for me? I broke my toe last night." Hough looked down at the toe, which appeared swollen and blue.

As everyone joked around before the game started, Hough could see some of the fleshy mural of tattoos on King's body. To her, King's defiant demeanor and bad-boy behavior was no different than on any other day. King openly bragged about one of his tattoos: "See my little nigger man hanging from a tree?"

Tommy Robinson, a senior investigator with the Jasper County Sheriff's Office, photographed the body of James Byrd, Jr. The twenty-five-year law enforcement veteran was keenly aware that some of his pictures would end up as vital documentation of the state's exhibits. He was selective, precise, and took his time, snapping crime scene evidence from every angle. Robinson took a picture of the dead man's dentures that just sat on the side of the road. There were other items in the human puzzle that also became part of the state's photo album. After Robinson pointed the camera toward a set of keys, already bagged as evidence, they were then taken to the victim's apartment. The keys fit Byrd's front door.

Other lifeless objects almost seemed to speak: Robinson took pictures of a left shoe, a can of Fix-A-Flat, a long-neck beer bottle, a sport shirt, and a tire track. Robinson snapped a photo of a nut wrench with the word "Berry" scratched on it.

First on the scene, Robinson arrived just minutes after a call from a Huff Creek resident. The unreal setting gave credence to an initial thought Robinson shared with Sheriff's Deputy Joe Sterling—that a large animal had been dragged. Another caller to the Sheriff's Office had described it as a "hit and run." With gloves and delicate steps around evidence, Robinson continued to photograph the Piney Woods landscape.

A week before the crime, Louis Berry borrowed his brother's stepside truck and log chain to clear some trees. It was physical, lumberjack-style work on the other side of neighboring Woodville. King and Brewer needed money, so they agreed to help. The front left tire had been punctured when Berry rammed something pretty hard while they were in the woods. The tire, which had a slow leak, was changed for the shabby spare. Already beyond salvage, they decided the best insurance was a can of Fix-A-Flat, at least until a more dependable replacement could be found or purchased.

After the bumpy wild ride the old truck withstood Saturday night, the front left tire finally ran out of air late Sunday afternoon. Before it was parked for the last time on the side of the Twin Cinema and the raggedy spare went completely flat, Berry's truck made one more short but crucial junket. King and Brewer headed to Tommy Faulk's house.

The part-time musician lived just one mile from the Twin Cinema on McQueen Street. Faulk had known his good friend "Bill" King since he was ten years old. Thick woods behind his house and a huge hole provided the backdrop for years of playing paint ball with the Berry brothers and King. Faulk had seen King change drastically after his release from a two-year stint in state prison: "He didn't like blacks and he didn't want to be around them." But even with the knowledge that King was a changed man, Faulk could not completely sever the adolescent connection.

Sometime after 5 P.M., Faulk, a twenty-five-year-old construction worker, arrived at his trailer home after a long and enjoyable day with his family. Faulk was not back from the outing thirty minutes before King and Brewer arrived unannounced. They parked Berry's truck off to the side, which was unusual to Faulk, as was their suspicious entry through his back door. Though he had known Brewer only a couple of weeks, he noticed there was also something amiss in his behavior.

After ten minutes, King and Brewer abruptly left. Neither told Faulk that they had just used an old hole in his backyard, approximately 75 feet from the trailer's back door, to conceal with a big chunk of earth an unusual murder weapon.

About ten of Jasper County's best investigators settled in for a meeting with the sheriff, who was now certain it had been necessary to contact the FBI and seal off the crime scene area, which on a Sunday could encounter heavy foot and vehicular traffic. Shell-shocked officers began to discuss "patterns" of known felons or troublemakers. But this crime just didn't make any sense; it was too vicious and could not have been committed by anyone from Jasper. One contradictory piece of telling evidence—the work tool with "Berry" on it—couldn't be ignored. In a town with fewer than 10,000 people, it wasn't a surprise that almost everyone in the meeting knew who the Berry brothers were, but no one could figure which might be capable of murder.

An unidentified witness came forward and provided a major break in the case: He saw James Byrd, Jr., riding on the back of a step-side truck a few minutes after he had passed Byrd staggering in the road drunk. He also told investigators that he was sure there were *three* white people riding in the cab of the truck. For obvious reasons, authorities did not release the name of their eyewitness. It would be stupid to take unnecessary chances while a murderer was still free. This man may have been the last innocent person to see the victim alive. He gave authorities a time line to work with. They now knew Byrd was alive for several hours after a relative's bridal shower. And they also had the grocery store video that provided a time for his final purchase. It clearly showed Byrd leaving.

Investigators continued to discuss possible suspects, but none of them seemed capable of this crime. In particular, they studied clues that might lead them to anyone who drove a step-side truck. An interesting set of names emerged, as well as the small apartment complex where several guys hung out, drank beer, and partied. One suspect was employed at the movie theater. As serious discussion about Shawn Berry kicked into high gear, Berry himself proceeded with an artificially busy Sunday schedule.

By the time King and Brewer returned from Faulk's house, the raggedy spare tire spit out its last breath of air. After the gray pickup was parked on the side of the theater, Berry examined the truck and began to entertain possible options for a substitute tire. A few minutes later, about 6 P.M., theater employee Christina Smith showed up for work. Instantly, she noticed her boss's truck wasn't in its usual parking space and that the front driver-side tire was missing. Smith was told Berry had gone to the Exxon station to have it repaired, or to buy another, because there was no spare.

Berry returned with Christie Marcontell. They were in a white Grand Prix. Berry hopped out and quickly replaced the tire. Everyone waited to hear more news about the dead black man and whether the police had made any arrests. Berry described to Smith the nature of the crime. "That's pretty sick," he concluded. Smith did not say much; it was hard to focus on his provocative commentary about the method used to kill the victim. Her concentration was squarely aimed at Berry's wrinkled attire—he wore the exact same clothes from the night before, when they both worked. Smith denoted jumpy movements and gestures. Berry couldn't seem to sit still. He told Smith he had to run King and Brewer back to the Timbers Apartments and then take care of some errands. Later Berry returned, alone. Then his roommates showed up again with King's girlfriend, Kylie Greeney. It was a lot of back and forth: from the apartment to the movie theater to the car wash, from there to the apartment to the theater, to play volleyball, to Tommy Faulk's and back to the theater, then to the apartment and theater again, and, finally, to Exxon and a return to the Twin Cinema with other stops in between. All the while King, Brewer, and Berry ran around the heart of Jasper, investigators continued to discuss the fact that Berry happened to drive an older-model step-side truck.

Just after 8 P.M., Louis Berry was back at the Twin Cinema. He saw his brother in the lobby with King and Brewer. This time a pretty girl named Courtney Miller was with the older Berry; they all stood around a few minutes to chat. Shortly after, King and Brewer left with Berry and Miller. All the hasty arrivals and departures made the theater parking lot seem more like a bus depot. It was a quandary to seventeen-year-old Christina Smith. She wondered why King was so uncharacteristically quiet and why Berry was in such a constant rush to keep in motion. Berry suddenly announced he was hungry and wanted to get something to eat. Smith watched Berry leave. He never returned. Around eight forty-five Sunday night, June 7, Shawn Berry was arrested.

One of the most wanted men in Jasper history was quietly pulled over for an expired inspection sticker on his truck.

Larry Douglas Pulliam, former local police officer, had recently become a DPS trooper. Like all the law enforcement officers in the area, he knew more than a few people who wanted to talk to the man whose scrawled last name on a set of work tools somehow connected him to one of the most heinous crimes in modern history. Pulliam also knew that a few of those people headed to Jasper were from the Federal Bureau of Investigation.

Soon after he pulled Berry over on U.S. Highway 96, Pulliam discovered that Berry's driver's license had also expired and that the young man could not produce proof of insurance. Three strikes made it easier for the trooper to do his job: "You have the right to remain silent. . . ."

Without any mention of the unsolved murder, Pulliam released the pickup to officers at the scene and drove his new prisoner to the Jasper County Jail. A handful of the officers arrived straight from their strategic-evidence meeting. Berry did not contest the arrest, nor did he have any questions about why six officers appeared to help arrest someone accused of such petty offenses. Somewhere deep inside, Berry must have realized that three minor traffic infractions were the least of his worries.

After Pulliam escorted Berry to the one-story jail, Jasper County investigator Curtis Frame and a detective from the Jasper Police Department, Rich Ford, took possession of the truck. Before it was touched, Ford brought over a witness to see if he could identify the vehicle. Steven Scott told Ford he believed it was the same truck he had already described from the night before, the same kind James Byrd, Jr., was riding on. Ford and Frame first spoke to Berry at the jail. The suspect had little to say, even less to offer. The two men again read Berry his rights; he acknowledged full understanding. Without being coerced, Berry then freely granted Frame and Ford legal consent to search the truck.

Frame immediately noticed what appeared to be blood spatters on the undercarriage of Berry's vehicle. Upon closer examination, he found that pieces of human flesh were actually lodged in the truck's side and chassis. The worst-possible scenario came together like a bad dream. An astute graduate of the FBI Academy, Frame carefully collected sample after sample. Dirt and vegetation that strongly resembled the kind from the Huff Creek area were visible in places on the truck. Not all of the evidence, inside or out, was thoroughly cleaned up or buried.

Frame continued to examine the old Ford from headlight to bumper. Inside the cab, gloved hands did not have to search long before Frame came across tools that matched those found at the crime scene. Both sets had the same unmistakable etching to identify the owner: "Berry."

When Frame considered mounting evidence against the frightened young man waiting inside the Jasper County Jail, it was hard to believe that Berry, a mostly petty offender who occasionally drank too much, could possibly be involved in what he could only assume was a reprehensible hate crime. Yet authorities realized the owner of the step-side truck, and now their prime suspect in this case, ran around with a known troublemaker who bragged about all the racist tattoos he got in prison.

Before Frame and Ford confirmed that Berry had been living

with John William King, the apartment on West Gibson was already under surveillance. Not long after Berry's arrest, officers prepared to question any of the roommates who lived there. They did not even make it to the outside staircase that led to the second-level apartment. King and Brewer had just emerged to make a run across the street to Wal-Mart. Officers politely approached the two men and asked if they would "voluntarily" come in to answer a few questions. King and Brewer agreed. They made another request: Would it be possible to search the apartment? Consent was given. A suspiciously large quantity of presumably stolen meat was discovered. As night finally fell on one long day, all three suspects were reunited, in separate cells, as inmates in the Jasper County Jail.

Authorities definitely knew King, a frequent burglar, by way of escalating reputation, but Brewer was a complete stranger. After a background check, they learned disturbing things about the town's visitor. The parole violator was from Sulphur Springs, Texas, and had arrived only three weeks prior to the murder. He and King appeared to have a lot more in common than either man did with Berry. Both served time in the Beto I Unit of the Texas Department of Criminal Justice, and both were released in 1997.

Beto is not a nice place. Most offenders are young men in their twenties. If new transfers from county jails cannot adjust to the "gladiator" unit, if they do not establish themselves immediately, these inmates will be viewed as weak. Ready to provide free training are tough, hardened Beto inmates, acting as a sort of welcoming committee. In some cases, they pay a visit in a matter of hours. If a new inmate does not fight, have protection, or choose sides, he might find Beto a hard place to survive. Beto is where King and Brewer first met, the place both men acquired their prison art—racist tattoos that, at a glance, indicate dangerous allegiances and warped beliefs.

Around 11 P.M., Sheriff Billy Rowles called the Jasper County district attorney to provide an update on the arrests and to let him know that the three men weren't cooperating. The county's chief prosecutor, Guy James Gray, rushed over to the jail to consult with Rowles about a simple strategy the two law enforcers had used in the past.

As Frame and Ford continued to wear Berry down, Gray and Rowles discussed the case and the evidence, as well as which of the three men might be most willing to talk. It wasn't uncommon for multiple defendants about to be charged with the same crime to try to beat each other to a sweet deal. They knew the sheriff could only hold them on a possession-of-stolen-goods charge. King's freezer full of filet mignons and other goodies matched a number of items lifted in a burglary of an upscale eatery on the edge of town. About the same time Patrick's was hit, an establishment just north of the restaurant, Solley's Package Store, was also burglarized. The thieves took several cases of beer. Authorities could legally detain the trio only on these less serious, unrelated charges.

While Gray and Rowles watched through a one-way mirror, Frame patiently talked to his jittery young suspect. It was well after midnight. Berry was again advised of his rights. Frame battled fatigue and tried a new approach: He showed Berry some of what had been recovered from the crime scene. Like Frame, Ford knew that Berry would never confess unless he was sure they already knew what went down.

Frame dangled what Berry instantly recognized as his own property—the work tools with his name carved on them. Berry's facial expressions betrayed him. Fidgety, he had trouble breathing and moved to the edge of his seat. Berry got the shakes all over again, so nervous he was about to burst. Then Frame showed Berry the cheap lighter with the KKK insignia and the word "Possum" engraved on it. Through earlier interviews, Frame and Ford had already positively identified the person known by that nickname. Berry knew who the lighter belonged to as well, yet he remained silent about how the Zippo ended up at the crime scene less than twenty-four hours earlier.

Since Frame and Ford could not obtain a confession or enough information to ascertain who did what out on Huff Creek Road, the exhausted investigators began to lose patience with Berry. As their voices rose and anger replaced endurance, the sheriff stepped in to suggest both men take a short break. It had been a long, grueling day. They first got the call just after 8 A.M. on Sunday morning. Sixteen hours later, they had three suspects in custody but no confessions or charges. But one of the three seemed ready to break if investigators provided the first crack. Ford, a large man with giant hands and jet-black hair, had personally known Berry for many years and could feel something weighing heavy on his heart. Berry very much wanted to talk, to be free of his guilty knowledge.

Once Berry was alone inside the private interrogation room, Gray and Rowles decided to make their move. Investigators had primed Berry for the good-cop/good-DA assault. Both men went inside and explained, as calmly as possible, what Berry was about to face and what might happen if he intended to forever remain silent. Gray and Rowles had done this before. They knew that a suspect or criminal was more inclined to see the magnitude of the situation or understand the seriousness of it all when both the DA and sheriff showed up together in the middle of the night.

"Look, I know you've got a knot in your stomach so bad you can't sit still." Rowles stared at Berry. Indeed, the young man trembled and vibrated so hard the chair could hardly contain him. Gray took a turn. He remembered that Berry not only knew him personally, but he also knew his kids. Gray told Berry that he and the sheriff would not be talking to him if they weren't serious. Then he reiterated the fact that neither he nor the sheriff could make any promises, but that if Berry told them what happened, the knot would probably go away. Berry needed to tell *someone* before his nerves cut off his oxygen supply.

At first, Berry stuttered and stumbled, but he quickly found the equilibrium that helped him begin an official statement to the sheriff and DA of Jasper County. He started to breathe normally again, then explained that Byrd died because he was black and had made the mistake of accepting a ride from racists. Berry did not include himself in that descriptive category and denied any involvement in the beating, chaining, or dragging of James Byrd, Jr. Just before they stopped Berry to call the investigators back in, Berry told what was on his heart: "Hey, those guys will kill me if they can."

It took Gray and Rowles only about fifteen minutes to obtain the flawed confession that would finally allow them to move forward. It certainly wasn't perfect, but it was now after 3 A.M. and this was the major break they needed. Berry was now ready to give a signed statement to investigators. Curtis Frame wrote as Berry talked. In his first statement, Berry began, "I had nothing to do with it whatsoever." He outlined his movements after getting off work Saturday night, right up to his arrest on Sunday. While Berry gave his version of events, King and Brewer remained steadfast in their claims of absolute noninvolvement.

By the time Berry finished, investigators had seven separate statements on the record, statements Berry made without an attorney present, and without promises or coercion. Berry talked from the wee hours of Monday morning, June 8, to sometime late on June 10, when he finally took an extended break.

Frame not only recorded what Berry said and paraphrased some of it for the written record; he also made notes on discrepancies and inconsistencies in what Berry summarized. Frame told Ford, "While Shawn is in the mood to talk, let's just let Shawn talk." And so they did. By mid-June, the well of conversation had run dry.

Many of these same investigators and detectives had watched Berry grow up, counseled him on stupid mistakes, including a misdemeanor DWI charge in 1996. Or the time before, when authorities thought Berry had learned his lesson—a 1992 arrest for burglary with his good friend Bill King. Jasper is small, and there weren't many in town who didn't know the Berry name from one incident or another. Even the sheriff liked Shawn Berry and described him as a "good-looking boy" with a history of reckless behavior. Billy Rowles was among a key contingent that wanted to believe Berry. "His uncle and I are good friends, and I feel sorry for this kid." Berry, who expressed a drop of remorse but took no responsibility, was cooperative, visibly shaken, and dramatically different from the other two in many ways. But in a matter of hours, Berry's account began to fall apart.

Daybreak crept in. None of the previous twenty-four hours felt real to Billy Rowles. At first light, the sheriff left Jasper for the Beaumont FBI office, then played the few facts he knew over and over in his mind as he cruised down the highway. By the time he returned Monday afternoon, federal agents were already in place. And the parking lot at sheriff's headquarters was buzzing with reporters who wanted more information.

Initially, Berry told Rich Ford he didn't know where the chain was. By Monday evening, however, Berry not only accompanied investigators to Tommy Faulk's house to find it, but he walked, without hesitation, directly to the massive hole in Faulk's backyard where it was buried. Two agents from the FBI and Ford walked behind him, evaluating his actions and mannerisms. Berry knew from King and Brewer exactly where the log chain was buried. Investigators retrieved the accused man's property from a big depression in the ground, then escorted Berry back to jail.

After Berry finished his last statement to authorities, he did not provide any more details or information about the crime. He was through talking. They no longer believed, if they ever did, Berry's assertion that retribution from King and Brewer was one reason he did not help the victim, or come forward right afterward. Berry's story was full of holes. Authorities began to weave a stronger yarn that reeked of self-preservation. Their theory hinged on Berry's fear of discovery, not retribution. Any sympathy, along with his chances for a plea bargain, evaporated as Berry's story continued to unravel.

Three days after the crime, King, Brewer, and Berry were arraigned and charged with murder. The judge ordered all three held without bail. The impoverished trio made a request for court-appointed attorneys, but none stepped forward. Judge Joe Bob Golden found it difficult to make appointments since the usual volunteers who stepped up to defend indigent clients didn't want anything to do with this case. Eventually, local lawyers were persuaded and assigned to represent the accused.

Though the presence of an FBI-led, multiagency task force signaled a certifiable hate crime, Jasper officials continued to play down that aspect of the case. Sheriff Rowles summed it up at one news conference: "We have an isolated incident. Guys who are not our kind of people did some stupid stuff." But after documents were recovered from King's apartment that pointed in the direction of hatred and racist prison ties, there was little left to do but confirm to the world what others had already speculated on. Two of the three men in custody, King and Brewer, may have had ties to the Aryan Brotherhood. Authorities knew they met while serving time at the same prison unit near Palestine, Texas.

New information trickled in each hour. Jasperites were terrified. Black residents who had never supported the death penalty in their lives urged the DA to find a legal way to seek the death penalty in this case. Blacks in East Texas, particularly those in the Huff Creek area, were overrun with gossip and innuendo that other attacks against minorities were being planned. Sheriff Rowles even had to dispel a rumor that another black man had disappeared and was "missing."

Concerned parents dreaded leaving their children at home alone, even to run errands or go to work. The crime threatened to tear the community apart. Black and white families in Jasper that had gotten along for generations were afraid and suspicious of each other. Usually, such skepticism was reserved for outsiders, but with two white boys from Jasper accused of committing a cowardly act of racial violence, many wondered who they could trust. Tension forced a few black residents to strap on weapons to protect their families from what they feared was imminent danger. Or the KKK.

Prosecutors worked through death threats, relentless questions from the media, and a large shadow from the U.S. Attorney's Office. If the DA had enough evidence to pursue capital charges without offering a deal to Shawn Berry, it would mean charges under state jurisdiction instead of federal. Some worried that state charges might result in automatic maximum sentences of life. To go after the death penalty in state court, prosecutors would have to prove another felony was committed in the commission of the crime. A felony in the same league as kidnapping would be extremely difficult to prove. A witness had already placed Byrd on the back of the truck, apparently riding as a "guest" of three white men in the front. It did not sound like kidnapping. Federal jurisdiction could easily argue that Byrd's civil rights were violated during the murder, a textbook hate-crime case because of what happened on Huff Creek Road. Guy James Gray's sleepless nights were just beginning as he heard from people who wanted punishment meted out by Texas itself, those who would only be satisfied with Lone Star justice—capital punishment—more commonly referred to in Texas as "the stainless steel ride." All waited to hear the next move from the small-town prosecutor.

When Brewer's lawyer informed the ex-con of all the international publicity the case was generating, Brewer was stunned. He could hardly believe it. Public Defender William Morian told reporters his client was "scared as hell." Another terrifying reality for Brewer was his denied access to King. Though they could not verbally communicate, they knew through attorneys and the jail-house grapevine that Berry had attempted to cut a deal. King and Brewer began to send each other "kites," secretly delivered letters passed to one another by jail trusties in exchange for small treats like candy bars.

Before long, authorities drew blood, measured feet, and took photos of all three defendants and of each of their tattoos. Prison officials in Huntsville verified that King and Brewer were never members of the Aryan Brotherhood, at least not while serving time. They also confirmed that a few tattoos both men sported were signs of membership in a smaller group, the Confederate Knights of America (CKA), which, they told Jasper County officials, was a "clique" closely affiliated with the Klan. Berry had only served county jail time and boot camp, and had no such known affiliations.

Before King and Brewer were transferred back to state prison to await trial, Jasper County jailers noticed newly scrawled graffiti inside King's cell door. They found the words WHITE PRIDE and his prison nickname, POSSUM, as well as a bold declaration that left little doubt as to the strong feelings about his former friend.

King had written SHAWN BERRY IS A SNITCH ASS TRAITOR.

Part Two

A JOB TO DO

THREE

Stella Brumley fondly recalls the last time she saw her younger brother alive. She was visiting her family in Jasper and was about to return home when James Byrd, Jr., had placed his arm around her as he jokingly vowed to be on time for a planned Father's Day celebration at their parents' church.

Vivid images of her sibling, at the piano, playing the trumpet, or just walking away that Saturday as he said "I love you," flash through Brumley's mind. She can also hear the soulful baritone deliver his favorite, and now befitting, hymn, "Walk With Me, Lord."

After Byrd's only brother, Thurman, and his sister Mary Verrett match various-colored ties to five or six different suits they will let his children consider for burial, they leave Son's apartment and head to the Sheriff's Office for an update. The grieving siblings assume the undertaker will dress their brother for burial. When Billy Rowles learns of their mission, he is forced to step in. Publicity-shy Thurman Byrd, just arrived from Dallas, asks Rowles about the extent of his brother's injuries. Rowles says, with tears in his eyes, "Please don't ask me, because then I'll have to tell you." At that moment, the extent of Byrd's suffering becomes clear. He will not need a suit.

But the Byrd family tragedy is not theirs alone. An invasion of press corps ensure that their devastating news is broadcast throughout the world. CNN, Court TV, ABC, CBS, NBC, and Fox News all have national reporters at the scene. Others freelance for international operations. The Associated Press has dispatched several correspondents to cover any news on the defendants, family members, the town, rallies and protests, and Byrd's funeral. *USA Today, Life,* the *New York Times,* the *Houston Chronicle, U.S. News & World Report,* and many other world-renowned publications—all have their best writers in town, those sensitive enough to tread lightly and still get the job done.

Jesse Jackson arrives, genuine in his efforts to offer comfort to the Byrd family and townspeople. Before all the yellow ribbons for a peace rally go up, a string of dignitaries from every corner of the world offer their take on the senseless crime. Some Jasperites resent what they fear is meddling and "stirring the pot." Others believe that a few elected officials and various leaders who make statements simply seek the media spotlight. In some cases, the barrage of cameras and microphones unknowingly serve as platforms for attention to causes totally unrelated to the crime, causes spawned by radical groups, moneymaking schemes, and ambitious political climbers. Only a handful of gestures appear genuine, including one from the commander-in-chief.

President Clinton tells the rest of the nation that the slaying is "shocking and outrageous." He also personally phones the Byrd family and speaks with the victim's parents and his sixteen-year-old daughter. During their ten-minute conversation, the president offers heartfelt sympathy to the family and tells them how sorry he is that the tragedy has claimed their loved one. His attorney general, Janet Reno, promises that everything humanly possible will be done to bring the killers to justice. It gives the family hope amid a media circus rife with politicians and extremists.

Another extended hand comes from an unlikely source. NBA's poster boy for rude behavior, Dennis Rodman, offers to pay for Byrd's funeral. The basketball player has several Texas connections, including a mother who lives in Dallas and memories as a former player with the San Antonio Spurs. When Jesse Jackson informs Byrd family members of Rodman's wishes, they are deeply touched.

Many applaud the usually flamboyant Rodman for his decision to keep a low profile. Though he does not attend the Saturday funeral, plenty of other luminaries join Jackson, including NAACP Chairman Kweisi Mfume, U.S. Senator Kay Bailey Hutchison, Transportation Secretary Rodney Slater, New York minister Al Sharpton, Houston Mayor Lee Brown, and U.S. Representative Maxine Waters, chairwoman of the Congressional Black Caucus.

Before her journey to Jasper, Waters was joined in Washington by several colleagues, including two respected representatives from Texas: Congresswomen Eddie Bernice Johnson and Sheila Jackson Lee. The trio of black women stood proudly as fellow House members voted unanimously, 397-to-0, to adopt a resolution to send "heartfelt condolences" to the family. U.S. senators adopted a similar measure. James Byrd, Jr., in death, has finally gotten his wish—millions know his name and Jasper's much heralded place on the international map of hate.

At the service, a few flush faces look as if they might faint from the oppressive heat. Hundreds squeeze into Greater New Bethel Baptist Church and an overflow fellowship hall. Across the street, an armed march quietly begins that has officials and residents holding their breath—a Dallas group adorned in indigo berets call themselves the New Black Panther Party. The white-supremacist groups aren't far behind.

Well-tended foliage at the Jasper City Cemetery offers little relief—mourners try to stand in what little shade the trees have to offer. Others just outside the cemetery, on the street, reverently watch Byrd's coffin being lowered into the ground to the sound of sobs. Something is different. A subtle change, begun as a quiet gesture initiated by the Jasper Ministerial Alliance, inspired officials to tear down a wrought-iron fence that, since 1836, had kept segregation alive in the graveyard. Black dead were buried on one side of the fence, and whites on the other. Byrd has broken a color barrier for the deceased. Unfortunately, the significance of the absent fence is lost on the outsiders jockeying for position and agitating, largely, for the sake of cameras. It will take more than iron to keep them apart.

As an anchor at a Dallas-based affiliate of CBS Radio, the closest I come to the case was hearing graphic, firsthand accounts from shaken colleagues. For all of their shared and surreal information, I cannot feign gratitude. Nonetheless, the personal insight better prepares me for all the updates that must be written and reported.

As a news anchor, part of my job is to provide crisp, two-minute updates on a myriad of stories: murders, plane crashes, bank robberies, political coups, kidnappings, and now, a dragging. Though Dallas is only 250 miles from Jasper, it might as well be thousands of miles away. Safe in my living room, I watch television in shame as the Piney Woods drama unfolds in a community that bills itself as "the Jewel of the Forest."

A Monday evening rally for racial healing follows Byrd's touching memorial. Hundreds sing "We Shall Overcome" on the courthouse square. They listen to prayers, promises, and condemnations of the crime that has attached an unwanted stigma and burden to innocent Jasper citizens. My heart goes out to them, and to the Byrd family, but I feel tremendous relief that I will never have to step foot in such a place, one that is only fifty five miles north of Vidor, Texas, renowned for Klan protests over a 1993 federal order designed to integrate an all-white public housing complex. Many now consider Vidor the Klan capital of the state. All over East Texas, history has left documented proof of those who do not don robes and pointed white hoods but provide silent support of bigoted ideas just the same.

During the remaining days of June, I watch as Jasper residents live under enormous pressure. The once serene timber town now rests squarely atop a powder keg, while outside agitators—primarily white supremacists and black militants—dance around with lit matches. Another factor that adds to the already explosive volatility is Texas' scorching hot weather, with temperatures that have already reached a hundred degrees by midmorning. The potentially dangerous combination of six-packs to cool the wrong heads, the sweltering weather, and fierce outside agitation only provides delight for those hell-bent on destruction.

In a town where the mayor, the school superintendent, and the president of the Chamber of Commerce are black, citizens wait to see if the racial-healing message will stand. Mayor R. C. Horn admits his frustration but adds, "I am doing my best to keep the city together and not let the hate spread."

One rumor is confirmed—bold neighbors show up to hold their much-speculated-on "White Pride Rally." The program features an imperial wizard of the Klan, who is in Jasper to loudly "denounce" the senseless murder of James Byrd, Jr. Turnout is disappointingly low for a joint-sponsored rally. Two small Klan factions, one based in Vidor (Knights of the White Kamellia), use the opportunity to recruit. There are no long cafeterialike tables full of hate literature. But several of the twenty or so Klanspeople hand out business cards so interested "white patriots" will know how to reach them or log on to their Web site.

At the Democratic State Convention in San Antonio, Rev. Jesse

Jackson cited the Klan's need for an audience and offered a suggestion for how residents should respond: "People in Jasper ought to go fishing." It is hard to say if the advice can be credited for the rally's low attendance. There are no traffic jams or huge spectator crowds, with the exception of a large pack of newshounds. Cameras click and videotape rolls as journalists wait in the wings for a shot at the winner of a confrontation between fifty angry black men and the Klan.

Militant groups from Houston and Dallas converge on the peaceful rally to "monitor" the situation and protect African-American citizens. As Klansmen wave Confederate flags and hurl insults, a few militants try to storm through a barricade. They do not make it across. Others wait at the ready with what authorities can only assume are loaded shotguns and rifles, on the edge of a cordoned-off downtown. Inside the two-block radius, another attempt by the first group to reach scattered Klansmen forces a line of officers to shield their bodies, then brace for the rush. The black militants are turned away twice, and are twice as angry they cannot grab the whites taunting "This is Klan country" as they parade in front of the Jasper County Courthouse.

Former Nation of Islam spokesman Khalid Muhammad tries to incite the small band of curious to join in: "We can run over the damn police. . . . Who's with me?" No one in the crowd offers to act as backup. A retreat down the block is something of a relief to authorities, who nervously sweat in riot gear.

With shouts of "Black Power," the second group, kept away from the square because of their weapons, wait for Klan members to leave the protection of sheriff's deputies, Texas Rangers, police, and DPS troopers. As the white men in various-colored robes file out, militant opponents finally seize their chance for face-to-face confrontation. When one Klansman attempts to drive away, his car is rocked by hands that would rather bounce him. Helmeted officers are forced to again separate black and white. The Klan makes a clean getaway.

Michael Lowe, regional director for KKK operations in Texas, Mississippi, and Louisiana, sounded a little like Shawn Berry the day before the rally in his statement to the media calling the Byrd murder a tragedy. Lowe assured reporters, "We had *nothing to do with it.*" Even with the very real threat of physical violence and all the inflammatory rhetoric before, during, and after the rally, the two-hour showdown, amazingly, nets only one arrest.

The nature of the crime and its aftermath make me all the more grateful that I will never be so near such explosive hatred. For the next few weeks, I do not even want to say the words on the air, but providing fresh details on what has come to be known as "the dragging" is part of my job.

Two months after I first learn the name James Byrd, Jr., and just five minutes before the start of my shift on another extremely hot day, I am unceremoniously fired. After nine years of numerous awards, I am nonchalantly informed that the Infinity/CBS station to which I have devoted heart and soul will not renew my contract as an anchor.

For weeks, all I can do is replay those last fabulous minutes as a news anchor. The reason I am fired is almost laughable. KVIL wants to target a "younger audience." At the time, I was one of the youngest voices on the air.

Instantly filled with doubt, rage, and insecurity, unanswerable questions sprint through my mind. How long will I be out of work? What did I do wrong? Why me? In addition to these and the normal thoughts of despair, there is something else that eats at me.

The only news anchor of color on the air, I can't help but wonder if my termination was, in any way, racially motivated. My bosses deny the accusation and simply say, "Don't take it personal." But how can I not take it personally when my choice of a career is an integral part of my identity?

Five months later, pride and bank account diminished, I reluctantly take a job with a different radio station, but one that is owned by the same parent company that let me go—a sort of twisted little irony. The new sister station didn't even know I was available and would've jumped at the chance to have me earlier, saving me thousands of dollars, loss of benefits and vacation time, not to mention humiliation.

Not a day goes by when race isn't on my mind. Not because I'm obsessed with it, but because others are so willing to provide nasty reminders that I am out of my place. To counter negative stereotypes of black America, I've always tried to do programs that promote inclusiveness and racial awareness. In fact, two of the awards I won for KVIL pay tribute to the Martin Luther King Holiday and Black History Month. Both "The Dream Is Still Alive" and "Black History 101" surprised everyone with back-to-back awards from the Dallas Press Club in 1992 and 1993, in the competitive Best Documentary category. Media professionals, and the companies they work for, love the bragging rights that come with being honored with prestigious Katie Awards. Several school districts now use both winning programs as teaching tools. Though proud of the awards, I was just content to expose our mostly white listeners to something positive, a counterweight to the news stories they hear about how terrible life is in the black community—crime, drugs, teen pregnancy, unemployment, and a general lack of opportunity.

Three months before the world and I would wake up to the horrifying news about Byrd, I was intensely engaged in two other major projects, both designed to promote racial tolerance and healing. The first project, "The Hockey Lesson," was centered on the Dallas Stars, the National Hockey League team that moved to town from Minnesota. After former hockey great Bob Gainey read a letter I wrote, the general manager invited me to the Dr. Pepper StarCenter to present my vision to attract more black fans to the games. A die-hard hockey fan and an even bigger Gainey fan, I wanted to see the league embrace the idea of ice rinks in more predominantly black neighborhoods so children can be introduced to the sport early, not be intimidated by it. The meeting and presentation were well received. And Gainey, who at that time had five Stanley Cup championship rings, set up a second meeting.

Less than a week later, my roll continued as I sat across from Ron Kirk, the immensely popular first African-American mayor of Dallas, to ask that the city support a proposal I had written to bring different cultures together. Dallas is a very racially polarized city. It had taken six months to convince the mayor to even consider scheduling a meeting with a member of the largely distrusted media.

After months of badgering, he finally agreed. We got off to a rocky start, but we were soon arguing like two legal foes. The Jack Evans Institute for Racial Healing was named for a beloved mutual friend who happened to be a former mayor of Dallas. Though Jack was only a one-term mayor, he was a wildly popular businessman characterized by many as a compassionate visionary who left his imprint all over the city, including the world-famous Morton H. Meyerson Symphony Center. Just weeks before his death, at the age of seventy-three, we had agreed to work together on a book about a prospective model church with an equal number of black and white leaders to show unity in religion. Jack had even found the property where he envisioned the church of the future would be located. Now, I was proposing a tribute to Jack Evans in which over the course of one year the city would implement twelve ideas—one for each month—wherein the races would work together. At the end of the meeting, Mayor Kirk shook my hand and pledged his support to a "very creative concept."

After the crime in Jasper, I took a long, hard look at what I was working on and didn't know if I had the strength to see these and other projects through or if I even wanted to. Sadly, it seemed that all the hard work to enlighten and educate had been in vain. Despite my efforts and those of others, three alleged racists dragged James Byrd, Jr., to his death.

Swallowing my pride, I start my new gig, a demotion from my old anchor position, as street reporter for KRLD in January 1999. After a mere ten days on the job, the robust news director many call "Big Daddy" for his hatred of "mendacity," enthusiastically summons me into his office to mete out the first major assignment. Over veteran reporters clamoring to go, Jack Hines instructs me to pack my bags for Jasper, Texas. His excitement can be heard all the way down the hall above the noise of Wall Street bells, multiple interviews, and keyboards clicking at a furious pace. All the color drains from my face as I glare at Hines. I want no part of the upcoming February trial of John William King, one of the three accused in the dragging murder of James Byrd, Jr.

Hines swears he is not just sending me because I am black, but because he believes I will provide the "edge" he wants. But the last thing *I* want is to be in Jasper, to be thrust into the center of such a racially charged national story. Still bitter about being fired and then forced back under the corporate umbrella that pushed me out in the rain to begin with, I wonder if I can bring objectivity to this story. I instantly bring up the vigorous duties of motherhood, but Hines doesn't buy it. When I ask my new boss at KRLD if there is someone else he might send in my stead, he answers, "You da man."

On State Highway 63, I head east and crack open a window to smell something almost impossible to get a whiff of in Dallas—winter's fresh air. On the horizon, the strawberry-hued sunset melts into a touch of banana and orange that is splashed onto a canvas of blue sky. I can hardly concentrate on directions, so strong is the desire to admire this beautiful evening sky that wraps itself around Jasper. From 63, there is a right turn off the main highway that places my car on a deceptively isolated farm-to-market road that is simply marked FM 1408. The road is wide enough for two lanes and two cars. I travel at a pretty good clip, around fifty-five miles an hour. It takes only a few blinks of the eye for the small city to completely disappear. Less than two miles later, I am on the infamous Huff Creek Road. The sky, so beautiful only seconds before, now seems a bad omen, a willing witness to unspeakable deeds. I question, out loud, what is left of my sanity. I continue down the unlit, one-lane road that leads to a tiny wood-planked bridge. Just to the left of the wobbly bridge is an old unmarked, heavily wooded logging road.

To my immediate right, in between rows of towering pine trees, is an old raggedy floral print sofa with popped-out springs, an ancient television minus the screen, and other discarded items. I shake my head in disapproval that man's tattered trappings spoil such an appealing landscape. Logging roads exactly like this one are a part of my forty-acres-and-a-mule heritage. I just can't recall ever personally being on one, with the possible exception of a little dirt road relatives used as a shortcut to my Aunt T's house. These East Texas woods, kin for sure, remind me of those same Gloster, Louisiana, farm woods that still haunt me in crazy childish dreams, woods so dark it was impossible to see your own hand in front of your face. And now childhood memories merge with new fears.

Naïve enough to believe I'm up to the challenge, I pull over and start to walk the route taken by the murderers. Outside the security of a rented, evergreen minivan, I foolishly bend down to touch the ground where James Byrd, Jr., a man who could've easily been my own forty-nine-year-old brother, was first chained to a pickup and dragged for three miles. As I stand to thoroughly examine my surroundings, the wind howls a warning. When the wind rustles in the country, there are no tall buildings or sprawling suburbia to absorb its frightening whistle. I cannot help but hear it and know, without doubt, that it is time to leave. As if to confirm my instincts, a heavy darkness creeps in and leaves little light.

Seconds later, the picturesque sunset is subsumed into earth. Thousands of Texas crickets dutifully begin the nightly chirp. Despite the dark, something beckons me to go ahead. Against my better instincts, I take three or four curious steps, then slowly get down on my knees to check out what appear to be dark stains on Huff Creek Road. Only on closer examination, through thick gold-framed glasses, do I discover faded evidence rings left by investigators who circle items they find at the crime scene. It is easy to trace the former reddish-orange dusty circles with my index finger. Having researched the story before this trip, I'm familiar with much of the evidence. Chills run up and down my spine as I imagine the contents of the faded circles—Byrd's keys, his wallet, a baseball cap, a watch, and more.

Once it gets totally dark, I fight an intuitive, understandable apprehension that I cannot be out on this road, in pitch-black darkness with gory details of what has already happened to one person of color. It is time to go. It is still East Texas, at night, in the woods. I am more afraid than I have ever been.

As I turn to run back to the limited sanctuary of the minivan, fresh fear icing through my veins, I can only imagine what James Byrd must have felt like out on this road—outnumbered, overpowered, and all simply because of the color of his skin. At that moment, I stop hating the job I have been dispatched to do. I forget the blame game. I finally forgive those who fired me. The sorry search for excuses ends on Huff Creek Road.

On the way out, I backtrack so I won't get lost. I retrace all my steps out of the heavy woods, back to FM 1408, onto 63, and into the welcome light of the city. Back in the small hotel room, my hands continue to tremble. Clasping my right hand around the left to discourage the movement, I need a quick shot of whiskey or a long, slow drag of a cigarette to calm me down. I can't sit still, so flushed with the knowledge that after this excursion I will never be the same again.

Hard liquor is an almost foreign companion I rarely invite for a visit. But seeing the evidence markers on Huff Creek Road had a way of making strange bedfellows seem like appropriate associates. I can appreciate the opportunity to down a cognac, cheap rotgut, or anything else with a little kick. Jasper's dry status limits my options, and I don't know any of the local bootleggers. The closest I come to Jim Beam, Jack Daniel's, or even Yago Sangria, is a new bottle of Tylenol PM right next to a Bible in my still unpacked luggage.

A short time later, I call home to speak with my two children. The youngest grabs the phone first: "Mommy, are you coming home tonight?" As an anchor, I never traveled, and Brandon, who is only six years old, struggles with my absence. His big brother, Roderick, puts up a brave front and bombards me with a number of questions that clearly reveal how worried he is. Since he's almost sixteen, I cannot lie or get him to change the nature of his interrogation: "Can you eat the food, or will they put poison in it?" He continues with a second flurry: "Don't watch any movies that will upset you, and hurry home," and then, "Are they all racists, Mom?"

When my husband, Rod, finally gets his turn on the phone, he sounds weary. My guilt level instantly shoots up—I am not there to help Brandon adjust to all-day school and the challenges of first-grade life. One of his teachers sent home a note that Brandon is sullen and quiet and not sure if his mom will ever return. Rod does not want to tell, but I find out anyway that Brandon constantly asks for me and cries when he hears my voice on Dallas radio. The only way I can remain in Jasper is if my mother will hurry over from Shreveport, Louisiana, and hold down the fort. Luckily for the whole family, she agrees.

Drained, I get off the phone and begin my Jasper journal, a spiral notebook I use to record my feelings about this case. I write for a long time, long enough to soothe frayed nerves. Two Tylenol PM caplets can't hurt. Most nights, they work like magic. In a few minutes, I'm usually in dreamland. But for tonight, I have to dismiss the notion of sleep and instead settle for simply turning off my brain. I'm nowhere near successful; alternate images cloud my mind. On one side are the tear-stained faces of my babies. The other features James Byrd, Jr., and his incredible hold on me.

On the eve of the first trial, a chilly Monday afternoon, I prepare to do whatever is necessary to get inside the Jasper County Courthouse. But it's Presidents' Day. The hundred-year-old courthouse is locked up tight. I prowl around with fierce conviction, determined to find a way in.

The only people present are two men who fiddle with some wiring on the roof just above the main door and another man at the white gazebo, which resembles a covered carousel with a giant porch swing. I look up to stare at the two men on the roof, then back at the third, closer to me inside the gazebo. They work feverishly and don't even notice me. It takes a second, but I soon realize this is a last-minute security check. All the reporters have been hearing about the promise of airtight security for weeks and wonder how such a small town will pull it off.

Set to call it a day, totally exasperated, I turn to head back to the Best Western. But out of my peripheral vision, I spot a welcome mat that wasn't there before, a welcome mat with my name on it— a thick piece of carpet rolled up to keep the front door propped open. Some careless maintenance man left it there, tired of using keys to enter and reenter.

I start to inch up the sidewalk, closer and closer to the cracked door. Four steps later, I look over my right shoulder, all the while calculating the consequences of entering without the "breaking" for the mad dash in. Once inside, I look back out one of the small glass slits on the top half of the front door; none of the busy workmen see me. I zip through the unsecured, obviously unplugged and brand-new metal detector to revel in a successful covert mission. It is the first time I smile in Jasper.

On the first floor, I laugh out loud, positive I've committed Jasper's first real breach of security. A faint echo laughs back. Before I can fully bask in the glow of the undetected moment, I am startled by a clink of activity from a side door. Down the long, spacious hallway, directly in front of me, is a tough-looking lawman in a huge white cowboy hat. He has a key, jiggles it in the lock, and then looks straight at me just a few feet away. I freeze. Unfortunately, it is too late to run. Our eyes lock. I search my feeble brain for something logical that will explain my peculiar presence in an otherwise locked-down situation. The tall, blue-jean–clad stranger looks me over, first up, then down, like a nod of acknowledgment.

As he approaches, I catch sight of what appears to be a very big gun. I do not blink. Or breathe. My own knees threaten to knock me over. The gun is not nearly as shiny as a huge badge pinned to this muscular chest, which leads to the natural and stereotypical assumption that I am face-to-face with a good ol' boy, some kind of plainclothes ranger. As he gets closer, I fully prepare to spew out the tried and proven "I'm a journalist" trump-card speech. Suddenly, the unexpected happens. The heavily starched white shirt does a right flank, pulls out another key, and pushes his way into some office door. For several seconds, I am still too scared to move. I wait.

When my heartbeat finally slows down a little, I slither up to the door to read the words DISTRICT ATTORNEY. Since he neither shoots nor arrests me, I prance up to the second floor to see, walk around, and sit in Judge Joe Bob Golden's courtroom. Double doors lead to the same legal arena that will boast Standing Room Only in a matter of hours. After a quick prayer, I take a few notes, look at old black and white photos that line the wall, all white people, and touch as many objects as possible, all the while keeping a check over my shoulder to make sure I am still alone.

It feels strange to do so, but I sit at both prosecution and defense tables to boldly point a finger at the opposition. In my heart, I know it is the last time I will find peace in this space.

As I stand to stretch, my eye catches long-stemmed ceiling fans, that, though not present in the movie, remind me of the courtroom scenes in *To Kill a Mockingbird*. I fantasize that they will churn each day that testimony is given, that they will cool the flame of collective anger without extinguishing the call for justice.

I tiptoe back down the sturdy staircase to look for the man who disappeared into the district attorney's office. Noting the coast is clear, I run out of the Jasper County Courthouse as fast as I can.

A few hours later, at the first official media briefing on the courthouse lawn, I encounter the same man again. I look at him to gauge any indication that he might recognize me from earlier. There is nothing. He shows no outward clue and checks me out with the same casual suspicious look he gives all the other reporters.

Guy James Gray, the district attorney, makes the introductions and promises to answer all questions and tell reporters county rules. When he gets to the tough-looking white man with the perfectly shaped balding head and piercing blue eyes, I learn that the man I've privately nicknamed Wyatt Earp is actually the assistant DA, Pat Hardy.

After the media briefing ends, dozens of reporters are lined up with cameras to get live shots and tape with Guy James Gray and Pat Hardy. I do not speak with either prosecutor. Some of the other players, mostly from the U.S. Attorney's Office, are also besieged with interview requests. Jack Hines will never forgive me if I don't have fresh tape for morning drive live reports, so I stake out a spot in a long line of hungry news people. Because I work in radio, a medium considered a dinosaur by many, my position on the journalistic ladder is somewhere behind network television, print, cable news shows, and whatever else remains. I patiently wait my turn and grab at different people who can grant exclusives. My once aggressive reporter's ability to push inside the pack is buried somewhere deep under the anchor persona I try hard to shake. But instincts die hard. One thing is certain—I am not interested in interviews with a group of folk. I am determined to snag a one-on-one. As the sheriff takes a quick break between live television shots with six o'clock news reporters from around the state, I lean over and whisper, "Have time to talk with me when you finish?" The sheer subtlety catches him off guard; he assumes a pleasant expression to mask his fatigue. "Yes, ma'am."

Fifty-three-year-old Billy Rowles sits with me in the crisp evening shade on a black-trim courthouse bench. He's dressed in his customary Texas-size white hat, boots, and Wrangler jeans, with a plump, wrinkled jaw full of chewing tobacco. We sit more like two old friends instead of sheriff and journalist. As it slowly gets darker, it also gets nippier; it's February, after all. I button my lightweight jacket, turn to Rowles (pronounced "Rolls"), and stick a big microphone in his face: "What would you like the outcome of this case to be?" There is an uncomfortably long pause between us. Then Rowles thinks a minute more, with hands warm in both pockets, careful of his answer: "Justice for the blacks and the whites." I do not ask the obvious. Still, he can read it all over my face, *"Is that possible here in the New South?"*

When the sheriff slowly speaks about what happened to James Byrd, Jr., he has real tears in his eyes. Rowles is so pained when he talks about justice and punishing "these boys" with the full force of the law, it catches me off guard. It is also a surprise that Rowles is genuinely interested in who I am and where I live. He wants to make himself available to answer questions. His friendliness and likable personality make me deeply uncomfortable, for Rowles is the physical image of everything in a small-town Southern sheriff I am taught to avoid and pacify. Yet he is nothing like the racist lawmen who once carried a twelve-year-old girl and her entire family to a smelly old East Texas jail on a bogus traffic violation. I remember that girl was me when I question the sheriff. In this interview, Rowles comes across as a kind, fair, magnanimous man, one I sincerely like. It bothers me, goes against everything I was taught as a child of the Jim Crow South.

As we continue our discussion, I discover that big chunks of his longest day on earth are completely missing from a sketchy memory. "Have you purposely blocked parts out?" I quiz. He frowns slightly: "You know, that might explain why, and I have to be honest with you. I don't like to talk about, think or recall Sunday afternoon, June 7, 1998." As emotions surface, I feel a sharp tinge of guilt at all the probing questions that I must ask.

Rowles is finally able to speak of something he does remember from June 7, a lingering memory that has become a thousand-word picture in a string of frozen mental photos. "Their stomach had a big hollow spot in it as soon as they saw me, because they knew something was very wrong," he says, referring to the Byrd family. Sadly accustomed to his duty—the delivery of devastating news to loved ones left behind—the sheriff is quick to explain. "The most important thing you can do after you tell them is to stay—you don't leave."

On Sunday, June 7, 1998, Billy Rowles did more than follow his own best advice. As he wept along with heavy-hearted Byrd family members, the sheriff of Jasper County also offered a compassionate shoulder and a little reassurance: "We're going to find out who did this."

FOUR

In the beginning, his name was not John William King. Born November 3, 1974, in a suburb of Atlanta, Georgia, the baby boy was named for his biological father—a man he would never know.

After a nasty split, the baby's mother left him with close friends in another state. It was understood by all parties that the arrangement was temporary. By the time the little tyke was three months old, it was clear that he belonged with the Kings. They offered stability, loved the child deeply, and were able to persuade the birth mother to give him up. The father showed more reluctance, especially since the child bore his name. Eventually, he was persuaded to sign away parental rights.

For Ronald and Jean King, who lived in Picayune, Mississippi, with their other three children, it was a time to rejoice. They renamed the child John William King. He completed their family of two daughters and now two sons. It did not bother the couple that many years separated the smallest King from his three siblings. The sister closest in age was already sixteen years old.

With all the legal paperwork set, the proud parents finally took little John to court when he was about nine months old. His patriotic red, white, and blue shoes captured the attention of everyone. John was a beautiful baby, a blessing sent just for them. A judge's signature made the boy a legal and permanent member of the King household.

When the child was nearly two, Ronald King left Mississippi and moved his family to a small Southeast Texas timber town. In fact, the home where John would run and play was right near Louisiana Pacific, where his father secured employment as a millwright. John, soon nicknamed "Bill," got along with children of all races. The neighborhood where the Kings lived was integrated, one of many selling points that made Jasper a more tolerant community than most of its East Texas neighbors. Folks worked and lived together, side by side, well aware that subtle racism existed mostly in economic terms rather than cultural barriers. One of his closest friends was a little black kid from the neighborhood.

Bill King was considered a bright boy who did well in school. By all accounts, the quiet child seemed to soak up knowledge. There was nothing unusual about his upbringing. He not only received an ample amount of love and attention from his aging parents, he also enjoyed the affection of surrogates. His older sisters got along great with him—sometimes acting more like fussy young mothers instead of siblings. His brother had already left home, but he too doted on the family pet. There was no doubt that John William King was deeply loved.

"Oh sure, I spoiled him," his father now reflects. "I woke up telling him everyday how much I loved him." The frail voice breaks. The elder King recalls how his son had one friend in particular that "he was just crazy about." The friend was black. Nothing in his background jumps out as preparation for a child who would grow up to become a die-hard white supremacist accused of a horribly violent crime.

"Oh no, I loved him to death and was proud to take him out in public," King sadly states. One of the best memories King has of his son was his lack of annoyance over displays of affection. "He was never embarrassed about being hugged, he believed in showing us that he loved us."

A religious foundation in the Baptist church kept the younger

King grounded and in touch with his salvation. As a well-mannered kid, he did the normal things boys in a small town were expected to participate in: church, school, and sports. "He was the kind of teenager who could be a role model for any teen. You'd want to show him off to anybody," the proud father reminisces. But he says his wife and daughters kept certain mischievous incidents about the boy from him. His eldest, a grown son in the military, warned him not to spoil the family baby. King says he later discovered there were little things his son was accused of—like broken windows and skipping school. For the most part, he chalked it up to sowing a few wild oats. After all, his son wasn't so different from other boys he ran around with. They were all the benefactors of clean-living and hardworking parents. His was a lifestyle consistent with that of a country boy.

King insists that "Bill knew his personal views" on race and respect, for he not only taught the teenager right from wrong, he demonstrated fairness and equality by the company he kept. Ronald King boasts of having close black friends, and two black goddaughters that his son knew about. He did not mention to his son, however, that another family member once also stood trial for a hate crime—long before the term entered the legal lexicon.

In 1939, Ronald King's older brother and another man were accused in the murder of a forty-nine-year-old traveling salesman in another state. King's brother and codefendant used as their defense the man's alleged sexual preference—they claimed he made a pass and attacked them upon being rejected. The two men were never convicted. King is adamant that the full story was only unearthed because he shared the basic facts with a reporter, who in turn betrayed his trust. Unhappy that his entire family continues to be measured by something that happened when he was just a child, King blames himself for making what he believed were off-the-record comments. He explains that in his brother's version of the story, as it was told to him, "when they left [the victim], he was alive. They had all been fighting."

Other things were printed, broadcast, and repeated about King in the aftermath of the James Byrd, Jr. murder, things he says are not totally accurate. Some of the Jasper locals interviewed by FBI agents were once employed at the same lumber mill as Ronald King. A couple of former coworkers told authorities it was not uncommon to hear King use racial slurs as a younger man. More disturbing was an allegation that King openly bragged about membership in a Mississippi Klan group before moving to Jasper more than twenty years ago. A weary King denies any truth to the story that he once belonged to the Klan, adding, "There were plenty of others to rebut what was said by just two people." He is not exactly sure why former coworkers sullied his name. "It doesn't bother me that they were telling lies to investigators about my past and about comments I didn't make; it was something they felt they had to do." At sixty-seven, King is in a wheelchair fashioned with an oxygen pump he must keep with him at all times. Prior to the trial, he almost never used the chair. Constant stress, his emphysema, and the probing investigation into his private life now demand he use it daily.

When John William King lost interest in his education, trouble became his tutor. A few odd jobs around town could not hold his interest either. First, he was caught breaking some windows at an industrial facility near his home. Jean King paid for the damage without alerting her husband. Other things were also shielded from the man who calls his son the most loved boy he knew, his "favorite child."

In 1992, things plummeted downhill for the younger King. When he was sixteen, the only mother he had ever known died. What he didn't know was that Jean King's brother had once married a woman with a daughter from a previous relationship. That daughter, though no blood relation to the family, was John William King's biological mother. He had no contact with her, and now he had lost the one woman he truly loved. With the tender barrier between King and his father gone, a once hidden side came to light. The teenager was caught burglarizing a building.

Suspended for "dipping" (chewing tobacco), the tenth-grader chose to pursue adventures that kept him connected to friends with whom he had more in common. At seventeen, King and a new running buddy, Shawn Allen Berry, were arrested with a third accomplice and charged with breaking into a building. In the fall of 1992, Berry and King were sent to a Sugarland, Texas, boot camp.

Ninety-day sentences actually seemed to help both. King's father remembers that he would sit outside the courthouse, waiting for his son to report to his probation officer. To keep tabs on the young burglar, state officials assigned him ten years of mandatory probation meetings. At the time, the elder King didn't realize that many of those planned dates were simply skipped by a clever kid who would just dodge around the courthouse, then appear again in time to facetiously exit.

While King believed his son was "special," others saw nothing extraordinary except the great speed and determination with which he ran down the wrong path. It led straight to the Texas Department of Criminal Justice (TDCJ) and a notoriously violent state prison unit called Beto I. After King violated the terms of his probation, he earned an unwanted promotion to Beto in June 1995.

As Ronald King struggles with a degenerative condition and all the medication he must take, including methadone and morphine, his heart continues to break for a boy he cannot save or find the will to abandon. "You've got whatever kid you get," he coughs, in between gasps for air. "You don't stop loving them."

True to his philosophy, King accepted his son with open arms and few questions when the young man returned to Jasper in 1997 after two years in Beto. King says he never liked all the tattoos his son came home with, but was told it was just part of some culture the newly muscular stranger studied while in prison.

According to TDCJ records, King did switch his religious affiliation from Baptist to Odinist, something he never took the time to fully explain or define for his father, who remains confused about its theological origins. Before Vikings converted to Christianity, many believed Odin was the all-powerful god of battle, wisdom, knowledge, and poetry. Odin was the father of a more popular god, Thor, ruler of strength, whose symbol was the hammer. Odinism supports the theory that warriors must be prepared for one final battle against evil that will ultimately end in the destruction of the world. They believe it is an honor to die in such a battle. The old man did not completely understand the spiritual conversion, nor the external one that accounted for black ink all over his son's physique.

Rebel flags, a swastika, lightning bolts, and terms such as "Aryan Pride" dumbfounded the elder King. He could not fathom what prompted the decision to get so many, including a baby Jesus with horns. His son no longer resembled the small, shy kid who weighed only 140 pounds when he left home. King admits he was disturbed at first, but nothing could overshadow the joy he felt at the return of his son.

For a time, things seemed normal. John William King convinced his father that the racial tattoos were nothing more than "prison art," something he had done to show how proud he was of the white race and his new religion. Behind bars, King attained some computer skills; he had already earned a GED from Angelina College before his stint in state prison. He even talked about a job where he could work outdoors, perhaps put a talent for construction work to good use.

A few job applications later, King reconnected with Berry, the best friend who had answered none of the four letters he wrote to him from prison.

Helen Brewer is a very religious woman. She spent her life teaching three sons and two daughters the difference between right and wrong. For many of their formative years, the petite brunette was left alone to serve as both mother and father. Her military husband, Lawrence, was stationed at foreign bases for more than a decade. No one will ever know how much of an impact the absence had on the Brewer child named for a heroic father with whom he never got the chance to bond. When the senior Brewer briefly returned, the family moved to Cooper, Texas. The reunion didn't last long. Another tour of duty swept the career serviceman abroad. And he was off again. When the head of the family finally returned to the States, the Brewers packed up and relocated to Kentucky, where they lived only a year. Finally, the Army veteran retired and moved his family to Klondike, Texas.

Settled now in Sulphur Springs, Texas, it is beyond difficult for the brokenhearted mother to understand how one of her five offspring could possibly stand accused in the dragging death of another woman's son. Devastated, she tells the Associated Press, "I couldn't do a dog that way. That just shows you what alcohol can do."

From the time her son, Lawrence Russell Brewer, was born in 1967, Mrs. Brewer always did the best that she could by her second child, and all her precious charges. Money was tight and life at a bleak Army base was tough. She was, in fact, a lonely wife with only a ring and five children to show for the union. Out of necessity, the married woman functioned more like a single parent scraping by on government paychecks.

All the years Helen Brewer spent holding down the fort with five young children, she was a kind and loving mother who worked long hours to nurture and train. She raised her children to know God, and did an admirable job under the circumstance of desperately missing a much needed husband. So long without him, the permanent return proved a difficult transition.

Like his mother, Lawrence Russell Brewer, called Russell by friends and family, is small in stature and shy. Both exhibit timid personalities. Having a larger-than-life father built like a locomotive and nearly six feet tall was intimidating for the boy, who was sure he would never measure up to the decorated Vietnam War veteran. Still, he tried to get to know his father, to please him.

Instead of dad and his namesake making up for lost time, the elder Brewer apparently ruled with an iron fist. There was tension and the minor problems associated with adjustments to life with a wife and five children. Doug Barlow, who would eventually take over as the defendant's lead attorney, knew from his close work sessions with the family that Brewer was a strict disciplinarian. But Barlow says there was also another side: "From what I know, he was a compassionate, sincere and caring man." The Beaumont-based attorney believes Brewer's military training probably meant he expected others to "tow the same kind of line." Indeed, a certain toughness in the senior Brewer revealed that sorry excuses or weakness would not be tolerated.

All of the Brewer children were described as "good" while they were growing up, including Russell, who was extremely protective of his mother. In court records, Helen Brewer agrees with the assessment, and expands it to include her spouse as a "good daddy," who, according to her later testimony, "drank some on the weekends." After her husband's twenty-year military career ended, Brewer continued to be a solid provider, affording his family the comforts of a middle-class environment.

Despite better economic conditions, at age twelve, Russell needed guidance. His mother steered him toward positive activities. He sang in the church choir, played with friends, and had the love of his siblings and other relatives once the family settled again in Texas. But he started experimenting with drugs as a teenager.

Like King, Brewer had childhood friends of all races and lived in a mixed community. No one thought Brewer academically gifted. Suffering from low self-esteem and fear of the unknown, he started skipping school. His dad soon found out. At fourteen, Brewer was kicked out of the house and not allowed back. The senior Brewer, afraid that his other children might be corrupted by a wayward sibling, would not take the chance their brother might influence them to dabble in drugs or skip school. Homeless and afraid, Brewer turned to new teachers with unsavory street resumes. He dropped out of Cooper High School.

No matter what he did, Brewer could always convince his mother to help him out with spare change, food, and clothes. Even with secret support from a loving mother, he had to abruptly leave whenever his father showed up, because the eviction could never be lifted. A difficult parental decision, it was meant to teach Brewer to grow up and become a man. The snap judgment haunts the elder Brewer today, as he can't help but wonder if things might have turned out differently had he continued to provide a roof for his son to live under.

Desperate to support himself and his growing drug habit,

Brewer demonstrated a willingness to change. He did odd jobs. At seventeen, he returned home and joined the National Guard. Fleeting admiration over the manly decision gave Brewer a small shot of confidence. But other habits continued to whisper his name. "The drugs is what led him astray," his mother would later testify.

Brewer sunk so low that he targeted the homes of family and friends to burglarize. As he stole, a lot of sympathy for him evaporated. No matter how far astray he went, Brewer could always return to the loyal mother who consistently encouraged him to do better. When his strict father was at work or out running errands, Brewer sporadically returned like a beggar at the back door of his former home. Helen Brewer would later recall a conversation in which her son was so distraught he cried, "Which way, mama, which way do I go?" As she is known to do, the righteous woman advised her son to read the Bible to find an answer.

Certain bright spots in his life made it seem that Brewer would not give up on himself. He got his GED from East Texas State University in Commerce. Brewer also held a few jobs, though none for very long. It was a feeble attempt to show critics who cast him off that they were wrong. Unfortunately, other stuff kept getting in the way of Brewer's efforts to redeem himself.

That "other stuff" became part of a disturbing record the state of Texas began to document. In October of 1986, Brewer was sentenced to seven years' probation for a burglary in Cooper. Not quite a year later, he was arrested in July on the same charge. Because Brewer violated the terms of his probation, he was briefly sent to prison. It should have taught him a lesson. In early 1988, Brewer was paroled to Cass County. Old habits gave chase. When authorities slapped the cuffs on Brewer in March 1989 in Snyder, a marijuana charge netted him ten days in county jail. Chance after chance, Brewer could not seem to function in the outside world.

On April 28, 1989, the small-time burglar and drug user finally hit the big time with a fifteen-year prison sentence for cocaine possession. Brewer swore to his family the drugs, at least in that case, were not his. He agreed to take the rap because the man he was living with "was doing drugs."

Paroled two years later, Brewer made more attempts to turn his shattered life around. In one lockdown, Brewer went through a rehab program. He sought more meaningful employment to make something of his life and support a new family. In 1993, Brewer married a Hispanic woman from Fort Worth named Sylvia Nunes, the mother of his infant son. They hardly enjoyed a honeymoon at all. His parole was revoked later that year. Brewer was immediately sent to the Beto I Unit of the Texas Department of Criminal Justice. The odds were no longer in his favor. Brewer entered prison under the worst possible conditions that a white man can—being an attractive, small, nonviolent offender with an unassuming personality.

Born two days before Valentine's Day in 1975, Shawn Allen Berry's childhood was hardly sweet and the hand he was dealt hardly fair.

Although born in Jasper, Berry and his family lived a stone's throw away in Kirbyville. Around age three, Berry's spirited young mother, Kathleen, took off. Neither parenthood nor marriage could fully tame the adventurous personality Berry had always heard stories about.

Though Berry was raised by grandparents—a grandfather and step-grandmother—the man his mother had married continued in the role of father to young Shawn. In 1990, Berry moved back inside Jasper city limits to live with his maternal grandmother, Faye Berry.

As a child, he had flourished in his country boy status. His grandparents had a large fowl farm where he could keep busy with lots of work and wide open space. They had chickens, cows, and a few horses. Deer and other game coexisted in nearby woods that Berry loved to run through. He was a rugged child who participated in just about every sport school had to offer. Except basketball. Berry thought he was too short to master the sport of hoops. But he reveled in football, track, and anything else athletic. Like a lot of adolescent boys, his sports career began with Little League baseball.

Preferring the outdoors to the inside of a classroom, Berry nevertheless tried hard to build mental skills and master school. But eventually education seemed a waste, taking time that could be spent doing more productive things. While he lived in Jasper, Berry continued to go to school in Kirbyville. Berry grew up well loved and nurtured in what he considered a normal environment. But what happened in 1990 can hardly be classified as a regular family occurrence.

Donald Hopson, the man Berry considered to be his father, committed suicide on a secluded patch of land owned by his family. Today a daughter owns the property off Huff Creek Road, just before the old bridge that bedecks the same creek and predominantly black neighborhood where Berry used to swim and play. It is located right near an old dirt road they all used to walk down— the same one on which James Byrd, Jr., would end up chained to the back of Shawn Berry's truck.

Berry was crushed. Hopson, the man his young mother loved before she hit the road for Alabama, was the only father he had ever known. Berry knew who his biological father was but had never met him. In Berry's mind, his real daddy was gone. First, a woman who gave him life abandoned Berry when he was a toddler for whatever selfish reasons. Then, a man he deeply loved shot himself. No matter what he did, Berry could not keep his head up.

Berry's spirit, along with any desire to remain in school, was broken. When Berry's grandmother was away at work, he would skip school. Behavior problems and low self-esteem did not afford the boy a wealth of choices. Before ninth grade, Berry called it quits and never looked back.

Faye Berry vigorously lectured her grandson about the merits of a good education and the potential it would bring for a decent future. Berry would listen, let her believe he was in school, and go straight to work. To the fifteen-year-old, work was way more important than what some stuffy old schoolbooks had to teach. With no experience necessary, Berry got his first job at Church's Chicken.

In school, and on the job, Berry counted black people among his slew of friends. He was the life of the party wherever he went and comfortable enough with blacks that a few from the baseball team once spent a night at his house. His grandparents raised Berry to understand the meaning of equal treatment for all.

Berry's social circle grew when he got a second job sacking groceries at the H.E.B. Pantry. There was nothing left over once his grandmother paid bills, the rent, and scraped up enough cash for food and clothes. Berry did not want to depend on her totally because he felt old enough to carry some of the weight. They were poor but proud. Berry knew that if he wanted things beside the necessities, he'd have to find better-paying jobs than Church's or H.E.B.'s.

For the first time since Hopson's suicide, things for Berry looked up a bit. He became a jack-of-all-trades, dabbling in construction and concrete work. Aggressive and willing to prove his manhood, Berry sometimes worked seven days a week. Grown-ups say he was a quick study who mastered all types of skills. William Sparks, the man who eventually became Berry's longtime probation officer, remembers his reckless charge often wore two faces. "He was something of an enigma; he had a good work ethic and likable personality, but couldn't stay out of trouble." In his free time, Berry liked to do what a lot of country boys did—ride around and raise Cain.

Berry's reputation came to the attention of law enforcement early. They knew about the regular brawls and other juvenile behavior. One woman recalls how Berry and his brother Louis would ride around to "case the town." Any misdeed or trouble was nearly always preceded by a joy ride. Something to break the monotony.

One night, Berry was just out riding around town in his car, shooting the breeze over the CB radio. Everybody had gone CB crazy with the good-buddy, ten-four lingo utilized by truck drivers and made popular in country songs. Berry was having some technical problems when he heard a confident voice over the CB airwaves who bragged that he could fix radios. The anonymous teen gave Berry directions to his house; he went straight over. Instantly impressed with the large home-based system, Berry watched the new friend talk up a storm on his CB radio.

True to his word, the young man repaired Berry's radio on the spot. To Berry, sixteen at the time, John William King seemed far wiser than his seventeen years. Sparks recalls how Berry was completely enamored: "There was something about King that drew Shawn to him; they were different. Bill couldn't stay focused on anything, but Shawn would stick with something. I don't know what he saw in King; maybe it was wine, women, and song." Whatever it was, the pair immediately started to hang out together. For a time, they were inseparable. Some even say they were best friends. It didn't take long for good times to turn into bad memories.

Berry's older brother, Louis, had also met King through a mutual friend. Sometimes Berry lived with his brother, which is where he was the night King and another friend casually dropped by. With nothing else to do, Shawn Berry left his brother behind to go riding with his two buddies. Minutes later, Berry was listening to plans to burglarize a machine shop where King worked. Someone had purposely left the back door to the building open. All they had to do was go in and take what they wanted. They settled on cigarettes.

Instead of saying no, or just getting out of the car, Berry not only rode along, he went inside. The trio never had a chance. Police were everywhere; the place was surrounded. Berry hid. But detectives knew two people had gone inside while King waited in the car. Seems police had received a tip about the unlocked door too. Berry soon gave himself up and lost all he had worked so hard to accomplish. His education continued at boot camp.

Caught red-handed, Berry coughed up all the details about the botched crime in his statement to police. Berry got a plea bargain out of the deal. Tight-lipped King and his coworker went to court. Despite Berry's cooperation, he and King received the exact same punishment: ninety days.

Returned to Jasper for second chances, King's father helped both young men get jobs working for Louisiana-Pacific. Berry stayed. After two weeks, King quit. Berry discovered King was not only lazy, but that the friend he once admired over the Citizens Band radio couldn't stay out of trouble. More problems eventually forced King to go live with his sister in Vidor. It gave Berry a chance to think about all the mistakes he'd made. Soon a pretty young woman had Berry thinking about other things, including love and commitment.

Christie Marcontell was a beauty. Not only did she hear it often enough from passing strangers, but she also had the trophies to prove it. Miss Newton County saw something in Berry that made her give him the time of day. With long auburn hair and doe eyes, the beauty queen knew she could wrap the roughhouse around her finger. Aware of each other for years, they finally had their first official date. So smitten was Berry, he informed his probation officer in 1995 that he wanted to marry Marcontell. "Shawn came in here one day and told us Christie was going to be in the Miss Texas pageant," William Sparks chuckles. Sparks thought Marcontell's presence might calm the rough tide. "A lot of guys I see, they slow down when they find a serious relationship. Not Shawn; King kept coming around."

Berry had finally secured the love of an attractive woman who could help build him up and restore the lost confidence. With Marcontell in his life, Berry's hard edges did soften a bit, but the two were not immune to arguments about his philandering ways and bad-boy tantrums. For a little woman, Marcontell could loudly "discuss" toe-to-toe with Berry and stand her ground. As the disagreements added up, Berry continued to make time for extracurricular hobbies that included chasing women and riding bulls at the rodeo. Berry was enjoying a full life of being in love, holding down multiple jobs, and joyriding on back roads. To avoid trouble, and jail, Berry tried hard to stick to the terms of his boot camp release. Sparks was there to help: "I remember telling him not once, but *several* times, to stay away from Bill King."

Berry saw King one final time after a scheduled meeting with his probation officer. King came barreling up to Berry on the sidewalk, desperate for a ride. To Berry, he seemed in a hurry, like he was running from somebody. Berry was trying to keep his nose clean. He left King to fend for himself and returned to work. Shortly afterward, Berry heard King had been caught and sent to state prison for parole violations. For a time, Berry was free of King. But then the first letter from prison came. He showed it to his good friend Heath Johnson. Berry had no interest in responding. Then the second letter arrived. By the time the third piece of mail from Tennessee Colony was delivered, King was advising Berry to "stay white" and using prison slang like "bro," something Berry didn't like, or understand. He threw all four of King's letters in the trash.

One day at work, Ronald King came to see Berry with a camera. He suddenly snapped a picture and said "it was for Bill." Since Berry would not write back, King got his father to send the next best thing to prison: a picture of his good friend.

Something happened to John William King at Beto I. He will not discuss it. Just hours after he was processed, assigned a number and cell, prison records indicate King was involved in some type of scuffle. Speculation persists that King was beaten, sexually assaulted, or both. Whatever greeting he received from the infamous Beto welcome wagon, it is generally agreed that King's attackers were black.

Not long after that first day, King met and drifted toward Lawrence Russell Brewer, who offered him protection in the Confederate Knights of America. Months earlier when Brewer first arrived, he was "checked" by two Hispanic gang members.

All the inmates in Brewer's cell block had been ordered to sit down on benches in the break room or they would be punished by guards. Blacks took one bench, Hispanics occupied another. The remaining whites would not let Brewer sit with them on the last bench, so he was forced to lean against a wall. It became his permanent position for two days whenever his cell block was allowed out for recreation.

Asked whether he would fight or "ride," Brewer refused both, but acknowledged his preference for a beating rather than give up money or sexual favors, which is how most gang members "check" the strength or weakness of a new inmate. Whites, or "woods," who watched the exchange liked what they saw in the tough little man and decided to invite Brewer to join the CKA. Fearful of what might be waiting around the next corner, Brewer instantly agreed.

After a written document was signed to show loyalty, Brewer cut his thumb and pressed his bloody right print to seal the agreement. In the Oath of the Rebel Soldiers, Brewer solemnly swore before Almighty God and "these Klansmen here assembled" that he would bear true allegiance to the sacred principles of Aryan racial supremacy.

Four paragraphs later, there is even a shred of understanding for lost Anglos: "To my racial Brothers and Sisters from among the white community, who will hate and persecute me because they have been so cruelly brainwashed, I, Lawrence Russell Brewer, pledge my patience and love."

Among the twelve bylaws adopted by the CKA is the following: MEMBERS WILL NOT SOCIALIZE WITH MUD-RACE. Near the top of the list was a rule that may have been the catalyst for many inmates who joined: HOMOSEXUALITY WILL NOT BE TOLARATED [sic].

A few months later when King arrived at Beto, Brewer understood much of what King was going through as the newest "minority" on a racially segregated cellblock. One side of Beto was well over 50 percent African-American. The white brothers— or woods—who stood up to intimidators were the only family that could help Brewer survive and make it out alive. The CKA even meant more to him than his own young family—a Hispanic wife and their son, both of whom he would readily deny.

With his rank as Exalted Cyclops, Brewer secretly recruited Texas Rebel Soldiers for the CKA. John William King made the twelfth member.

FIVE

On the approach to the site where King and Brewer met, cows munch grass near blocks of hay on the open range. Pigs are fattened for the slaughterhouse and returned in white packages as pork chops and sausage. A few horses, in excellent condition, are kept and ready to mount at the drop of a hat. Trained hunting dogs are cared for as well as any human who calls this place home.

A thriving industrial area employs an endless supply of men who have metal-sign skills. There is abundant work available for those willing, and it is extended without the confines of pollution, heavy traffic, or federal taxes. Except for the occasional odor of manure, the air is so sweet few can resist riding with the windows down to inhale the invigorating freshness.

Almost 20,000 acres consist of rolling hills, thick woods, and prime soil where anything will grow, including a vast array of tomatoes, sweet corn, squash, watermelon, and okra. Rich crop colors dot the landscape with green, yellow, and red; the sight of so many black faces in the field conjures up images of plantation life.

Nearly all the Anderson County acreage sits less than ten miles from a one-stop-sign town known as Tennessee Colony, Texas, where more than 13,000 residents live in close quarters. They are mostly urban inmates divided into five prison units of the Texas Department of Criminal Justice. Men of all races work together on several projects, including a pest control facility, a farm shop where hay is processed, a swine plant, and a nursery. Four of the five units—Coffield, Gurney, Powledge, and Michael—are located together but separately run. The last facility, Beto I, roughly consumes 3,900 acres alone, and is home to more than 3,000 inmates, or, as many in the system refer to them, offenders.

Except for these massive boarding houses and the reason thousands must stay in them, almost any Texan would be proud to own the lush green property. Technically, taxpayers do own it, under the guardianship of the State of Texas.

Approximately one hundred miles from Dallas, I wind down a paved but narrow two-lane farm-to-market road. Houses are few and far between, with one or two mansions that do not seem to belong. There is but one church on FM 645, which very much resembles FM 1408 in Jasper, the same farm-to-market road that leads to Huff Creek. The grassy parking lot at the Faith Assembly is empty.

Four or five miles beyond, everything a visitor needs to know about Tennessee Colony, Texas, is posted at the town's primary intersection. On one corner is the Tennessee Colony Recreation Center. Across the street sits a busy Exxon station with two pumps and a general store. A bright green sign with easy-to-read directions to all five prison units cannot be missed. The arrow to Beto points straight ahead.

Deeper into Anderson County, approximately three miles from the town square activity, is another asphalt road that leads to a huge facility off in the distance. Guard towers loom high above a cluster of ugly flat buildings surrounded by coils of barbed wire.

On the left side of the road leading up to the entrance are small sets of military barracks that appear to be wrapped with the dull side of aluminum foil. There is no movement, no sign of life. It is impossible to believe that anyone—let alone 3,200 men—calls this home. Things are quiet and still. Across the street, on the right side, even plant and animal life in the woods appears muted.

Up ahead, on the left, is the turn that leads to the entryway, where a large wooden sign greets visitors: WELCOME TO THE GEORGE BETO UNIT OF THE TEXAS DEPARTMENT OF CRIMINAL JUSTICE, as if the entrance leads to a wildlife preserve or picnic grounds. Two uniformed guards are posted; they demand to know the nature of all visits.

Inside the armed gates and past the entry sit a neat row of red-brick homes, three single-story duplexes on the right. These are for staff. The first house belongs to the Beto warden; the second is occupied by another warden. The other property is empty. At home, the warden may relax, but he is never free of work, thanks to a diagonal vista of the prison.

Unsupervised males in white pants and white shirts roam around—the first sign of inmate life at Beto. They are men on a mission, mostly black men, easy to spot in the white prison-issued standard uniforms. They walk fast, entering and departing a small frame building that could be for equipment, recreation, or living quarters for trusties. There are no obvious guards who monitor them, but a trained shotgun is probably pointed in their direction at all times from one of the two towers located nearby. Several wear matching white caps. There is almost no visor to cover faces from the blistering hot sun. One black inmate is on a small tractor; he rides back and forth in straight rows over the grass. He wears a satisfied smile.

A corrections officer is posted at the designated sign-in area. The entire front portion of Beto is mostly gray, like concrete, and flat with a mile of open windows that appear uniformly measured at twelve inches.

Without a photo-identification card, no entry to the prison unit is allowed. A large sign instructs families of the offenders what is allowed in and what is not. Purses never go beyond this area. Neither do cameras or tape recorders. Phone calls are made to verify visits. An inmate, possibly from the group of trusties, watches in silence as the corrections officer receives official confirmation to open this mysterious world to an outsider. The handsome black prisoner barely nods in kind to the slight tip of the head given.

On the FM road that leads into Beto, there is a sign that warns all to make sure their car doors are locked: HITCHHIKERS MAY BE ESCAPING INMATES. Opportunities for potential getaway or escape must be tempting and seem tremendous with all the thick woods and delivery trucks that stop here on a weekly basis.

A loud buzz indicates the okay to push open the first electronic gate, a chain-link fence with a door carved out of the twelve-foot-high metal barrier. "On the gate," a voice yells out. It must be pushed all the way closed before the second fence-door, only a few feet away, automatically hums, then opens.

In addition to the dainty flower petals of yellow and purple that give Beto's front yard some variety, there are brilliant reds and blues on a dozen windows on the right side of the building. The mirage of blended colors and backward shapes indicates these are stained-glass windows: the prison chapel.

Administrative offices at Beto line the right side after the entry, while a reception area takes up a part of the left. Another larger area is just beyond this one, complete with vending machines of chips, candy, and soda. Visitors wait here for permission to move forward. The warden's office is the third door on the right. Inside is someone who looks more like a retired ballplayer than a man responsible for the lives of 3,200 inmates. The warden is all business, no doubt a woodsman on days off. A small smile disappears from his face when he learns one of the posted rules has been broken. A forbidden microcassette recorder, even in the hands of a rookie visitor, is not tolerable. Wearing a gray shirt and starched khaki pants, a young corrections officer is assigned the task of tour guide. The warden takes the recorder.

Down the hall, seconds away from the administrative area, is the first of many locked doors. On the other side is the heartbeat of this entire unit, a place known as the Control Picket. The centrally located area houses all the keys and monitors radio traffic everywhere in Beto. It is a monumental task. All use-of-force equipment is here. Everything necessary to quell a prison riot or ruckus is within reach for officers trained to gather at the hub. Beyond the very next locked door is a foreign world to most law-abiding citizens, a world that assaults ears and other senses before there is one look at life inside Beto I.

The sign reads SECURITY IS NEVER CONVENIENT. All corrections officers understand it as the rite of passage to access beyond the somewhat secure Control Picket area. They are four words that serve as a wake-up call to personnel that it is time to leave worldly distractions where they belong—outside. This work is hard, it is dangerous. You never let your guard down. Never let the inmates see you sweat. Never turn your back. Suddenly, the door is wide open. It is time to follow the guide inside.

Beto is fashioned as one long hallway with a series of locked gates and iron bars. The whir of many voices, a few loud, mostly muffled, sound distinctly like one man. On the other side of the Control Picket, there is not only a feeling of vulnerability, but of exposure. My sole form of identification is taken away and left behind at the 220-Desk located at the Control Picket. Except to the female corrections officer who knows name, address, and Texas town of residence, a feeling of dangerous anonymity behind the walls of Beto is unsettling. But the CO (corrections officer) knows who to notify in case anything happens. And from the puzzled look, she probably wonders why anyone might need a tour of the unit named for Dr. "Walking George" Beto, a former warden who won respect for his reputation of spontaneously "walking and talking" with inmates and staff. His face looms large from the photo in the foyer.

At chow time, dozens of unshackled men are out of their cells and in the hallway, which is the length of three football fields, with the Control Picket situated in the middle of two monster sides appropriately named North and South. Before any offender is allowed to march to the mess hall, he is searched.

Metal gates that are normally locked are briefly left open for inmates to file through as they exit or enter for meals. They are fed at intervals by the various wings. It takes some time to feed all 3,200 men. One of the most intimidating things about Beto is its sheer numbers. It does not take a calculator to figure that white shirts outnumber the gray ones fifty to one.

Men everywhere move, and as they do, they make little or no obvious eye contact with their foreign observer. They are, at certain times, let out of human cages, without wrist bracelets, to eat, talk, mop, and socialize. In the barbershop, all chairs are full; four inmates cut hair. As the tour continues, a sea of faceless black and brown men pass by close enough for introductions and handshakes. Young and observant, the faces of a few white men who congregate together flash like a shuffled deck of cards. They too look down or straight ahead. Others take a peek when they believe it will not be noted. It is hard to miss such a sharp, bright contrast to the drab gray and cotton-white.

At the commissary, there is a long line. Men have but one or two opportunities during any given day to purchase items with money from their Beto trust funds. It is hard-earned cash deposited by friends and family on the outside. Most offenders are allowed to spend no more than $60 during any given period, which is usually about two weeks. Others, depending on their level of custody, are allowed to spend as little as $20 on various snacks and toiletries.

Exchanges occur through a small window where cash is accepted and items pushed back through. A dark black man grabs two loaves of white bread as soon as he pays. He moves quickly to place the sacred purchase in a dirty white bag with a drawstring. All inmates are allowed such a possession to shop with, or to keep their personal items stored in. Many carry them everywhere to avoid theft.

The six-year veteran responsible for safe passage calmly describes Beto as "a small city." Indeed, the resemblance is uncanny with the possible exception that this vibrant community is minus the normal presence of women and children. No doubt this unnatural lifestyle leads to a great deal of stress and pent-up frustration. Or high-testosterone clashes. The warden has no statistical information to back up complaints that indicate the heavily populated North is the more troublesome area of his little community. Fewer inmates are housed in the South, so it may be an easier place to do hard time—it certainly seems to many observers that fewer violent incidents occur here.

The southern sector is also where the chapel is located. A tranquil place, its painted tower of green and brown, strikingly similar to a guard watchtower, features a superimposed male figure with outstretched hands, pierced by nails. The palms of his hands are marked by crimson stains. It is the Christ, inviting, suffering, loving, and forgiving: artwork done by Beto inmates. Inside the sanctuary are twelve windows, the ones that can be seen by approaching visitors outside. Not authentic stained glass, the beautiful windows are nonetheless symbolic of each apostle's life.

Rows of ordinary worship chairs are slanted for the best view of the podium and stage. Though located in the southern section of the building, the chapel is a peaceful centerpiece of the unit, with easy access for inmates who choose to honor their faith. When not used for holy purposes, a stage behind the pulpit serves as an outlet for creativity. Hidden off to the left, just behind the makeshift curtain, are a set of drums, a piano, and a guitar used for special programs. Any solemnity at Beto is solely reserved for this time and space.

At the height of chow time, more noise and more men fill the long hall. The far end in the South is known as PRTC, a prerelease treatment center for offenders who are six months away from going home. The idea is to counsel inmates about to be sent back into the "free world" and help them understand what it will take to become productive members of society.

Known gang members live in F Wing, Administrative Segregation. The most incorrigible inmates in the prison population are housed in the Administrative Segregation wing and classified by three numbers according to behavior. A Level Three on Ad-Seg has more restrictions than a Level One or Level Two, even down to the amount of money he is allowed to spend. The door that leads to Administrative Segregation remains locked at all times.

All the Ad-Seg offenders stay in single cells that have a second set of black security panels across the first set of bars. They serve as square slots through which trays of food can be passed. Each six-by-eight-foot living space is equipped with sink and toilet. A large industrial-size fan strategically placed on each floor circulates what passes for a cool breeze. It is uncomfortable. Eight months of the year in Texas fall between warm and hell. Inmates know the only areas of the prison that have air-conditioning are the administrative offices, the medical facility, the school, and a handful of off-limit spots.

It takes more time and manpower to individually serve meals through slots for Level One, Two, and Three prisoners. Usually, Ad-Seg designees get only one hour out of their cells each day for recreation or showers. Every inmate must be strip-searched and cuffed before they are allowed outside the cell. An officer must accompany them to the showers or break room, and stay with them until it is time to return them to F Wing.

Back on the main artery, the north-south football field, it is busy as ever with more long lines at the only store in the vicinity—the prison commissary. A posted handwritten advertisement lists available stock. Band-Aids are 75 cents apiece. If an inmate wants a no-name laxative, it will cost $1. Fixadent is a whopping $4.25. There are no bargains or coupons to help drive down the purchase price. Money is a luxury that can produce daily struggles to maintain prized prison trust funds. While a few states pay inmate wages, Texas does not. Through an honest day's work in factories, fields, or offices, inmates earn credit for good time, which can be used to trim sentences. Very few Texans support the idea that prison is a paid job; it is enough that taxpayers must pay for "three hots and a cot."

An almost exact replica of housing and services is found in the northern section of the building. By several credible accounts, Beto's North Side is notoriously violent. Beto, like a few others, is known as a "gladiator" unit because the average age of most inmates is ridiculously young: mid-twenties. The dubious distinction is also a warning—gladiators either fight because they must or because they like to. In some cases, Beto gladiators are as young as seniors in high school. In a few rare instances, there are inmates near thirty. For the most part, they are young hellcats who hold life to be of little value, either the victim's or their own, and believe they must fight for respect, to protect and preserve what they have, or to take what belongs to someone else. Not all fill the bill. Those who do not, quickly learn what is expected by the state and the inmates who run the prison.

Back out in the sunshine of Anderson County, there is a kind of exalted relief. Above the brilliant silence, the noise of 3,000 voices is clearly heard, along with key clicks that secure metal bars. But there is another sound that I hear which these men cannot: the motorized hum of outside gates that offer precious freedom. On the way out of the prison complex, I notice a homemade sign in the woods: "Justice—swiftly, fairly, and evenly."

This is where John William King met Lawrence Russell Brewer.

"Up to three dozen new or suspected gang members in prison are identified in an average month," the corrections officer flatly states. Then, in a resigned tone: "The public has no idea of the level of gang activity throughout the prison system."

Texas is not just any prison system in the United States. It is one of the largest in the nation. Close to 150,000 inmates live in more than a hundred units that make up the Texas Department of Criminal Justice. The TDCJ is in a unique position to reinvent itself as a model system for others with similar woes. But progress is a slow and tedious climb from the basement, where Texas corrections officers suffer from low morale because their pay ranks forty-sixth in the United States for those who do this kind of work. Starting pay to risk their lives everyday is about $18,000 a year. Such salaries and work conditions often attract twenty-something high school graduates, who will get only four weeks of training to prepare for brutal twelve-hour shifts. Other statistics are even more sobering, and dangerous.

According to the TDCJ Security Threat Management office, there are more than 5,000 confirmed gang members in eleven security risk groups. Nearly 9,000 other inmates are suspected of allegiance or membership. Among the groups, which organize mostly by race, are some names familiar in the outside world. The Mexican Mafia is the largest. They have over 1,400 known gang members, and even more are suspected of support or membership. Five hundred inmates are confirmed members of the Aryan Brotherhood of Texas. An additional 800 may be secretly affiliated. The Crips are the largest black gang behind prison walls. Only a little more than 500 prisoners have been identified as gang members. Their real strength may lie in the fact that 2,400 others are suspected members who pledge life and loyalty to their cause.

No one knows the exact date that the problem of racist gangs first came to the attention of corrections officials, but one man, Salvador "Sammy" Buentello, has a pretty good idea. Several years ago, an inmate told Buentello a fascinating story about a prison gang in another state. "I sent him back to his cell and started making phone calls. I spoke to California officials. The more I looked, I started to see that some inmate violence was being perpetrated by gangs." It was the early 1980s.

Buentello and fellow employee Terry Pelz began to monitor different individuals and talk to them about their affiliations and beliefs. Since most of the gangs are Hispanic, being bilingual was certainly a help for Buentello, who is now an assistant director for the department that manages security threat groups. Pelz, who rose to the rank of assistant warden, is now a criminal justice consultant.

By 1985, one of the most murderous years in the history of the Texas prison system, 25 inmates were killed by other inmates. Buentello and a handful of others could see a dramatic link between the race of the victims and some of the slayings.

Before the year ended, officials took drastic measures to stop random inmate attacks and planned hits. Texas was first in the country to implement Administrative Segregation, a tool to separate and individually house offenders who have a propensity to disciplinary problems, those who require protection, and those who are security risks. Gang members, at some point, may fit all three categories. But most are placed in Ad-Seg because they belong to a security risk group.

Buentello's laid-back personality makes him a natural for his job. A kind of liaison between wardens and inmates, he will meet and identify racist gang members before they are ever issued a unit and number. First, prisoners are placed in a diagnostic area in Huntsville where they are put through an evaluation process, medical screening, family background, and other required procedures. Information is consolidated, and a determination is made on which unit an inmate will be sent to. Through this lengthy process, security managers are able to document an offender's gang history or suspected involvement.

As Buentello learned in his informal investigation, a group known as the Aryan Brotherhood can be traced to its prison roots at the California Department of Corrections in the early 1960s. Ex-convicts and inmates from San Quentin with white-supremacist beliefs demonstrated their take-no-prisoners style with a series of dangerous bank robberies and high-profile armored-car heists. Copycat prison groups immediately sprung up around the country.

Buentello soon confirmed that the Aryan Brotherhood of Texas was established after a group of inmates requested permission from California to form a chapter. Reportedly, permission was denied, but organizers went ahead with plans anyway to form the ABT. Eight of the eleven security risk groups in Texas originated behind prison walls.

Many, including the Aryan Brotherhood, the Texas Syndicate, and the Mexican Mafia, once lived by a particularly disturbing clause in their constitutions known as "blood in, blood out." In order to join the group, a potential member had to spill the blood of an enemy. "Blood out" literally meant there was no way out, other than death to the member seeking to exit the group. Today, it is harder to enforce the "blood in, blood out" old-school policy—a fact that does not hurt recruitment.

According to Buentello, several risk groups have ranking structures composed of captains, lieutenants, sergeants, soldiers, and a list of other well-defined positions. During its heyday, the ABT even had a steering committee that controlled illegal activity in and out of prison. No matter their race, almost all groups are motivated by control of the lucrative drug and sex trades through means of violence, extortion, and intimidation.

Another identified group, the Bloods, came into existence when founders Sylvester Scott and Vincent Owens formed the Compton Pirus, aptly named because the gang originated on West Pirus Street in Compton, California. Initially, the Bloods developed to protect themselves economically from the Crips, their traditional street rivals. Soon afterward, recognition given to the Compton Pirus rapidly spread across the country and other Blood chapters were formed.

Bloods, who identify with the color red, are one of the only prison gangs that can trace its beginning back to the streets, as opposed to prisons. Texas officials can confirm only 150 known members in prison. Close to 1,000 other inmates have suspected ties to the Bloods.

If security threat groups in Texas account for less than 4 percent of the prison population, and another known 6 percent are aiding them, how can such a small combined force control the other 90 percent? The search for answers has netted a varied set of opinions, but there is agreement that inmate violence plays a fundamental role. Easy targets are first made submissive, then turned into whatever is needed in the prison hierarchy: prostitutes, drug runners, bodyguards, etc.

Fifty percent of all Texas inmates are poor. As in the free world, they need money to survive. One way is through extortion. If an inmate is lucky enough to have a family member or friend deposit his allowed $60 to use every two weeks, he may be forced to spend all or part of it on protection. If that inmate refuses, daily beatings might help change his mind. Another persuasive method is the threat of prostitution. Inmates regularly use weaker prisoners for sexual services they can sell to those who have ready cash. A prisoner who does not fight off sexual advances is quickly labeled a "ho" and passed around. Sometimes he is even sold from one gang to the next. Even more threatening is the welcoming committee that almost always pays a visit to gang-rape the new arrival. At least once, a terrified nonviolent offender requested that medical services sew his anus shut.

Another lucrative option is an inmate partnership with a dissatisfied guard easily tempted by the lure of extra money. Texas employs more than 23,000 corrections officers who are, for the most part, hardworking men and women with pride in the uniform they wear. They do not see themselves as "guards." That term applies to corrupt personnel guilty of participation in illegal activity like smuggling drugs, tobacco, alcohol, and pornography inside for offenders to sell. Over the years, guards have been fired for lewd behavior with inmates, physical abuse, supplying contraband, and secret affiliation in some of the very gangs they are paid to keep tabs on.

According to Kelsey Kauffman, a national scholar and leading expert on prisons, corruption is a far greater problem among corrections officers than most officials will acknowledge. "Inmate activity is there because of a wink and a nod from corrections staff." Kauffman, herself once a corrections officer, calls American jails and prisons the most racially divisive institutions in the country. "Think about what you know about race relations in America," Kauffman urges. "If you take your most desperate African-American males and put them under the total dominance of white-run prisons, what do you expect to happen?"

Indeed, there is no quick fix, especially when evidence points to seven different states where prison guards have worn KKK insignia or posted swastikas to alert others of "open recruitment." In Florida, dozens of black corrections officers are part of two class-action lawsuits alleging discrimination. One black officer found the following hunting license in his office: "OPEN SEASON ON PORCH MONKEYS . . . Daily kills limited to ten."

Terry Pelz is also aware of state prison systems that have problems with corrections personnel. "In Ohio, some of the guards are members of the Aryan Brotherhood." Pelz says some racist guards stage fights between selected inmates. The internal strife caused by division among the ranks can wreak havoc in the life of a corrections officer. Experts say such officers have a higher divorce and suicide rate than those in some metro police departments.

Kauffman, author of *Prison Officers and Their World,* uses her doctoral dissertation from Harvard to make the point that racist institutions continue to be the South's response to the end of slavery. "In rural areas, where the prison staff is almost all white and they have very little cultural training or awareness, all the stereotypes about black people produce racism." Kauffman says it's not fair to the rural communities or the urban inmates who end up at the mercy of an insensitive white environment.

According to Kauffman, a number of employees, low-level as well as corrections officers, do stand up to say the behavior is wrong; some have even gone to the FBI. They are quickly singled out for harassment, threats, insults, and other forms of abuse. Many are forced to resign or seek transfers to other facilities. For fear of retaliation, many no longer feel it is worth it to speak out— especially when decent officers are cursed, attacked, maimed, and sometimes raped by angry inmates who lash out at a secret system of racial favorites. Kauffman believes a vital difference can be made by training and hiring qualified minority personnel from urban areas. But prisons have a tough time recruiting. Not many city dwellers want to live in the boondocks where units are located. Further, the idea of living with indifferent or racist neighbors does not encourage minorities to pursue such jobs.

Dr. Richard Watkins is one of the few black senior wardens in the Texas prison system. He helped to spearhead an effort to have his unit named for an African-American with a letter to then Governor Ann Richards. He smiles broadly: "Reverend Holliday was a community activist from this area. Holliday is only one of two units in the system named for a black man." Watkins believes if Texas is going to house so many black offenders, officials should also be willing to find positive black men after whom to name some of the units.

The native Texan is not shy about speaking his mind. Watkins has had his life threatened four times, twice by white staffers who worked for him. Because of his zero-tolerance policy on racist gang activity among corrections personnel, Watkins is known to ferret out troublemakers, like the rebellious officer who once wore a Confederate flag bandana on his head to work. Others remain silent sympathizers: "They have gone underground to avoid detection."

Of the United States district judge who put Texas prisons under federal oversight, William Wayne Justice, Watkins does not hesitate to say, "Justice is my personal hero. He forced the state to do what it should have done all along—employees to do their work and inmates to serve their time." Others do not share his view that the entire system needs to be overhauled. Critics blame Justice for destroying one of the most well-run prison systems in America.

Three major changes, all of them set in motion by legal action, forever changed the face of Texas prisons. In the transition, these sanctioned alterations also helped create an ideal setting for the rise of racist gangs. The backlash started with a 1972 civil rights lawsuit filed by an inmate named David Ruiz.

In the late seventies, alleged constitutional violations were aired in Houston court. In 1980, Judge Justice found that confinement in Texas prisons did constitute cruel and unusual punishment based on several factors, including brutality by guards, excessive force at the hands of "building tenders" (inmate-guards), uncontrolled physical abuse among offenders, and substandard medical care. Some prison officials are still bitter about decades of federal intervention but admit there have been improvements in staff and health care under Justice. Another lawsuit, *LaMar v. Coffield*, forced integration in prison housing.

Historically, Texas has always segregated inmates by race. All offenders—black, white, and Hispanic—would be placed on one cell block with only members of their own race. The policy of segregation insured against any serious interaction between the races. Even the workforce on prison farms was divided by ethnicity. In 1979, *LaMar* changed everything.

"Offenders were not happy about that [*LaMar* decision] and it caused a lot of racial tension," Sammy Buentello recalls. When officials complied, the results were a boost to security risk groups. "That's [the ruling] what the gangs used to actually recruit."

Whites found themselves outnumbered on newly integrated

cellblocks four to one. An imminent shift in power played upon the fears of those who perceived their status and positions of "privilege" in permanent danger. Reactions included more militant posturing as well as resentment over a new world order.

Another legal decision paved the road that would ultimately end what some viewed as preferential treatment based on race. Until 1979, black inmates had to run to the very fields where backbreaking labor was required of them. By comparison, Hispanics rode to work in trailers with backless wooden benches to sit on. Whites had separate trailers that not only included places to sit, but also support from backboards they could rest against. Black men saw inmates designated "building tenders" as little more than white overseers on the master's plantation. Others believed the inmate-guards were all institutional snitches who funneled information to prison officials about cellblock activity.

After Judge Justice ordered wardens to end the practice of already outlawed tenders, who technically worked for the state as unpaid guards, the prison system was ripe for a new kind of racism. Hundreds of corrections officers were hired to replace the ousted tenders. Millions of dollars were earmarked for new prisons. Medical services slowly improved. But integration wreaked havoc on white offenders who had little or no experience with black inmates. The proverbial upper hand was quickly seized in Texas prisons.

All the rapid changes opened the door for a new set of *invisible* building tenders: prison gang members. Black inmates suddenly found themselves in a new position of strength in the early 1980s. Many felt it was payback time. Their Anglo counterparts did not appreciate what they perceived as daily arrivals from the streets who had "attitude" and total disrespect for white inmates. Because the state-mandated power structure in prison collapsed, a campaign of abuse and hatred materialized through inmate correspondence and secret meetings. Against this legislative backdrop, the Aryan Brotherhood of Texas was born.

The roots of the ABT have been traced extensively and documented in the Fall-Winter 1991 edition of *The Prison Journal.* According to researchers, Mary Pelz, James W. Marquart, and C. Terry Pelz, whites who felt persecuted by defense mechanisms like the Mandingo Warriors or the Self-Defense Family, two black groups that organized in response to ABT tactics and extremist beliefs, found solace and support with like-minded whites who would risk life and limb to protect them. Inmate killings spun out of control.

One black was stabbed over accusations of "hogging" white inmates. Hogging refers to sexual exploitation or physical abuse. Another black inmate was killed by a white gang member who set out to prove his loyalty to his gang. And the list went on and on. Prior to the initial Justice ruling, annual figures for inmate murders were single-digit. In a matter of months, they tripled. In 1984 and 1985, suspected responsibility for a quarter of fifty-two inmate slayings were squarely blamed on the ABT.

As their reputation grew, more whites wanted in. ABT members became known far and wide as "mad dogs" or "crazy motherfuckers" who took their beliefs seriously. Watchdog groups list the original Aryan Brotherhood (San Quentin) as one of the most violent prison gangs in the country. A part of the ABT creed offers some insight into the philosophy of its members: "Death holds no fear; vengeance will be his through his brothers still here."

Prison officials fought back with their Administrative Segregation policy. Through communication and education, they armed themselves with as much information as possible about the ABT and other groups. Among a batch of confiscated written documents, authorities recovered a publication that outlined physically specific details on how to stab a black to ensure death rather than injury. It included a warning: "The smell of fresh human blood can be overpowering, but killing is like having sex. The first time is not so rewarding, but it gets better and better with practice, especially when one remembers that it's a holy cause."

John is an inmate who came to prison straight from the streets. Living fast and hard, the teenager soon found himself convicted of first-degree murder. There was no way out and no second chance; he had to pay for the life he snuffed out with a life in prison.

Nearly twenty years later, John savors every lesson he has learned about survival. For a huge chunk of that time, John was proud to be a member of the Aryan Brotherhood of Texas, a group he joined so he could have a family in prison.

"Basically, I joined the group because it was everybody helping each other out, at first," John recalls. But things quickly changed from the simple daily discussions about what the group hoped to accomplish to racially charged dialogue. Still John stayed connected because the ABT did offer help to others: "Somebody didn't have any family in the world, we made them feel welcome." It was a recruitment strategy that worked. Gang leaders knew if they flat-out told potential recruits that they were a bunch of racists doing drugs and arranging hits or participating in illegal activity, there weren't going to be a lot of folks signing up.

John claims he had few clues about the group's larger objectives because he never saw signs that the ABT was solely based on illegal activity with a racial slant. "It started turning racial around 1986, and that's one of the reasons I got discouraged with it." By 1989, John notes, "Everyone [all the gangs] wanted to be racial."

Though the groups align themselves racially while incarcerated, John is a firm believer that once members return to the outside world they either drop, or disassociate themselves from, beliefs adopted to survive. "ABT members are down with the cause as long as they are in prison," he says, "but when released, they forget all about everybody inside." Gone is the promise to financially and emotionally support brother inmates with money and letters. Some do send money back or share profits from criminal activity. But John never heard from any member in the free world when he was still in the brotherhood and has his own theory on why: "The hatred is a survival thing where everybody puts the white race down, or puts other races down. Naturally, everybody's going to band together with their own race for protection." Such behavior continues to play out in prison on a daily basis. John says it's a fact of incarcerated life. "Oh, it's widespread with events happening in each unit."

The ex–ABT member chalks up much of his experience to youth and ignorance about other races: "I wish I had never got in it because it ruined a lot of things for me personally. There were things that happened that I regret but couldn't stop." John refuses to say what those things are. But he was a member during the bloody prison uprising in 1984–85 when there were reported murders at several units.

Like the racist tattoo on his right arm, John's regrets are permanent. With his expressionless face wet with perspiration, John continues: "If everybody respected each other, not trying to run each other's lives and control everything, it might be better." John reveals his tattoo, then quickly covers it up with the short-sleeve prison white. "A lot of people do get them [tattoos] for protection."

Though tattoos are prohibited by Texas prison policy, inmates like John are able to get dozens of tattoos while locked up. Some are strictly for protection. Others send an indisputable message. If a white guy has three lightning bolts and a swastika on his neck, chances are he will not be approached by blacks for casual conversation. That's known as an obvious message. There are even tattoos solely designed to provide protection from sexual predators.

Some men—especially Hispanics—take an artistic approach to avoid being raped by another inmate, or worse, a group of inmates. Since the overwhelming number of rapes are committed from behind, a few Hispanic inmates have tattoos of the Virgin Mary etched on their backs. An attacker might hesitate in a fit of conscience over the sacred symbol. While a picture of the Madonna can give pause, a tattoo of a voluptuous female on an inmate's back sends an entirely different signal to a predator. Every offender, even those who choose sexually suggestive tattoos, must do what he can to survive one more day in the Texas Department of Criminal Justice. The corrections officers charged with watching over the inmates feel the same. Both sides agree that all most people want is a little respect.

Without it, prison is about control. Those with power exert it over the powerless. They are the inmates who decide what television programs will be watched in the break room, who has to pay extortion money, which inmates are worthy to be in their racist gangs. The 10 percent in control offer protection, dole out beatings, and battle over the sex and drug trades. The other 90 percent try to survive.

Experts say the whole prison environment means an offender, violent or nonviolent, whether he wants to or not, has to socialize to stay alive. Sometimes he joins a gang.

When it was first erroneously reported by some media outlets that John William King, Lawrence Russell Brewer, and Shawn Allen Berry were possibly members of the Aryan Brotherhood, all hell broke loose in Texas prisons.

"Blacks were very incensed," Sammy Buentello recalls. "They started to retaliate against white inmates, and then we started to have more racial incidents directed at the ABT," he says. Aryan Brotherhood of Texas members were also upset that anyone would dare believe that is how they would behave in the free world. The ABT defended itself against accusations and attacks, until a tit-for-tat situation developed.

As Buentello began a dialogue with certain individuals, he was convinced the dragging murder of James Byrd, Jr., did not fit the style or profile of what the Aryan Brotherhood is usually accused or convicted of. According to other officials who agree, the ABT would not be eager to do anything that would bring international shame, wide attention, or that particular kind of "dishonor" to the group. "When they recruit, they make sure of the backgrounds and personalities of the people they are recommending," Buentello says. The Aryan Brotherhood has never been a group any white man could just "join." It is more discreet. He must have a sponsor, a certified member who can vouch for his *character*.

John William King dreamed of being a member of the Aryan Brotherhood. But they are very selective. King may not have lived up to their list of high standards, which could explain why he settled for a lesser-known clique—the Confederate Knights of America.

A few months after his release from Beto, King finally had the satisfaction that Aryan Brothers everywhere took notice. Unfortunately for him, so did the rest of the world.

Part Three

DEAD MEN TALKING

SIX

The first time C. Haden "Sonny" Cribbs sat down to discuss strategy with his client, he had one question: "Do you want to live or die?" John William King did not like his options, or the sixty-year-old lawyer presenting them.

Easy to rattle, sometimes belligerent and uncooperative, King did not offer much assistance in putting together his capital case. At one point, Cribbs and cocounsel Brack Jones, Jr., made a request that they be allowed to withdraw. The motion was denied. Judge Joe Bob Golden ordered them to toil on.

They had endured the months of King's erratic behavior during jail visits, at which he might come out to talk to them or he might not. They put up with the shouting matches and abuse. They even made it through jury selection. Surprisingly, a softer side of their client emerged when authorities relaxed courthouse rules at jury selection so King could enjoy a nearly hour-long visit with his eighteen-year-old girlfriend, Kylie Greeney, and their five-month-old son, Blayne. It was the first time King had ever held the child he had only seen briefly at jail visits, a baby he refers to as "my little Viking."

And now the world waits for the twenty-four-year-old man to arrive at the same Jasper County Courthouse in which he so lovingly embraced his son before. Like the biological father King does not know, he too is an absentee father. An army of cameras and a throng of reporters wait to record his every angle, action, and reaction—facial expressions, gestures, words spoken, clothes worn, and anything else that happens in the course of this first "dragging trial."

Inside makeshift media headquarters located in the courthouse basement, it's a zoo. Several phones ring off the hook, all with questions about the man of the hour: "Has King arrived yet?" "Will he speak?" "How does he look?" There are long tables of equipment, food, phone lines, laptop computers, and speakers that pipe in every word from upstairs.

At ground level on the Austin Street side of the courthouse, mostly television crews and reporters are lined up behind two sides of yellow police tape to see King escorted into the courthouse. It is time to watch and record the defendant's first steps to justice.

Chilly, this is the Texas version of winter: cool, crisp, around sixty degrees. It won't be chilly long. For now, I turn up the collar on a flimsy all-weather coat and wait for afternoon warmth. The media contingent make small talk as they eagerly anticipate the defendant in the lead story of the American moment. Nearby, law enforcement voices on two-way radios coyly identify the prisoner, the clandestine route, and the estimated time of arrival. One code word produces some predictable jokes—"Possum," King's prison nickname. Five minutes later, cameras begin to click away.

As promised, security is extremely tight. The sheriff and company drive up onto an elevated, cordoned-off portion of the west side of the courthouse lawn, right up to a side door, where King can be easily whisked inside without too much commotion. King, helped by several plainclothes deputies, steps out of an unmarked police vehicle. Reporters pounce on King as soon as someone confirms it is the defendant.

While he looks straight ahead with a silly smirk on his face, some do what they are paid handsome salaries to do—yell questions, insults, and statements designed to elicit any response at all from Jasper's clean-shaven, neatly dressed CKA poster boy. "Did you kill James Byrd?" "Are you a racist, Bill?" "Why'd you do it?" "Any comment?"

We pack of journalists are quite a sight—a rapacious mob that some of the lawmen think is a little humorous. Deputies caution us to hold all questions, keep quiet, and stay behind the tape. "Leave King alone," one official loudly warns. Perhaps he has never dealt with urban journalists before. The threats are taken with a grain of salt. "Bill," someone yells, "are you guilty?" Every reporter gathered here would love for King, an icy, emotionless young thug, to spit out more of the racist venom for which he has become famous. It would make excellent copy. Millions are dying to hear what hatred this young sounds like. King stares straight ahead as if on some invisible red carpet with roped-off Hollywood photographers who beg him to look in their direction. King knows he is the center of the universe, and by the semipleased glow on his face, the last thing he will ever do is break the silence that whips so many journalists into a frenzy.

Death threats make it necessary to protect the accused, which explains the use of code words and covert conversations about which way the caravan will approach the courthouse. King proudly wears a dark navy bulletproof vest and appears smaller than he looks on television or in photos.

Slightly pudgy around the midsection, there is something almost charismatic about his doughy white face, his juvenescent features. The smug confidence of a young Klansman is frightening, for there is no hood, no sheet or burning cross. All the things that can warn a black, brown, or Jewish person that they're in harm's way have been removed. Of course, the revealing tattoos are strategically covered by a long-sleeve shirt—no need to frighten jurors on the first day. To see King's tattoos must instill the same kind of fear earlier generations felt at the sight of loyal followers of Confederate General Nathan Bedford Forrest, one of the original Klan founders from Alabama.

The young hatemonger takes the last three or four steps to a small landing, an almost porchlike structure. King plays with the media, answering no questions and providing no satisfaction. With his wrist bracelets barely visible beneath a folder he carries on top of his cuffed hands, King is ushered up the concrete steps without incident.

It is Tuesday, February 16, 1999. Fourteen jurors are escorted inside Judge Joe Bob Golden's courtroom. To the relief of many observers, a young black man sits on the panel. After they are sworn in, Judge Golden issues a deserved swipe at the media as he instructs apprehensive jurors that they must not watch coverage on television, listen to the radio, read the paper, or hold discussions about the case with anyone. Golden, with his fatherly face, looks at each juror. "I hate to refer to it as a circus." Yet, he decides not to sequester them from the impending tent spectacle outside. Eleven whites and the black man look grateful. Two alternates hear their names and acknowledge them.

Moments later, the capital murder indictment against John William King is read in open court. Opening statements do not take long. District Attorney Guy James Gray simply promises to let the evidence speak for itself, to tell the story of what happened early on the morning of June 7. When it is Sonny Cribbs' turn, he has no opening remarks, which in itself is a statement. It seems to say there is no defense.

First witness for the prosecution is Sheriff Billy Rowles. On the stand for an hour, Rowles relates in painstaking detail what he found on Huff Creek Road on Sunday, June 7, 1998. About eight-twenty that morning, the Jasper County sheriff was on his way to play golf in Dallas when he turned around and headed home to investigate an accident. Rowles glances at the jury, never wavers, and very calmly states, "Upon arriving at the scene, my units had just found the head of James Byrd."

By his own admission, Rowles mistakenly believed that if he simply backtracked a trail of clues, the information would lead to a possible arrest. It didn't take Rowles long to understand that the evidence suggested something far more sinister than a complicated hit-and-run. Rowles tells the attentive jury some of the tracks were not made by tires: "I knew that someone was being dragged behind some kind of vehicle." Rowles then carefully explains there were two sets of tracks, "coming and going." He tells of keys, shoes, clothes, and a music CD, all sprinkled like random confetti.

Of several pieces of gripping evidence at the scene, one produces a loud gasp among spectators. It is the first of many. Rowles and his investigators found a set of dentures and drag marks off the road. "I took a cap that I was wearing at the time and set it down by the dentures." The testimony drives members of the Byrd family straight from the courtroom.

High bushy grass along the road makes it virtually impossible to conceive that a hit-and-run accident could cause such a massive amount of trauma. "The place where we found the first footprint is where we found more tracks and a nut wrench." Then Billy Rowles turns to face the jury. "At that time, I believed we had a murder case."

The well-worn nut wrench, a common household tool, had the name "Berry" engraved on it. Further down the road, investigators recovered several pieces of evidence, including a billfold with identification inside, beer bottles, cigarettes, a Zippo lighter, a watch, a cap, and other items. As the sheriff examined the crime scene with his eyes, careful not to touch or disturb crucial evidence, he dubbed one area "the fight scene" because, in Rowles' own words, "several people are obviously in a fight." In his mind, a headless black body, an apparently vicious fight, and the KKK insignia on a cigarette lighter could mean only one thing: "I knew somebody had been murdered because he was black, and I thought that was a hate crime."

Before the sheriff is excused from the stand, he identifies a photo of the victim. Prosecutors do not show the picture in open court. When Rowles looks at it, he grimaces.

Defense attorneys vigorously object to graphic crime scene photos about to be revealed to the seven men and five women who make up the jury. Prosecutors respond with equal tenacity that the photos are necessary to show motive and intent. Adamant that the grisly color pictures will help prove the state's case, Gray apologizes to jurors for what he now asks the Court to let them view. King looks indifferent. Judge Golden overrules the defense objection; jurors take a deep breath.

In the media section of the courtroom, directly behind Byrd family members, there is a hush as all heads turn toward the jury box, located just to the left of the first two rows, where all six of the victim's sisters wait for reactions to the photos.

Across the aisle, curious spectators sit in thirty reserved spaces on hard wooden benches. They share the defense side of the courtroom. Before this moment, no one knows how prosecutors plan to present the explicit photos in public. As soon as members of the state's team stand at the edge of the jury box behind their table, it becomes clear. Fourteen black folders are passed, one to each individual juror and the two alternates. The strategy is simple—never show the photos in open court.

Jurors look down and open the folders to the first page. More apologies are made about the chilling evidence contained inside ordinary classroom binders. This jury has been warned beforehand against showing any feelings. None of them are able to follow instructions as hearts give way to reaction.

The pained faces of the jurors, men and women alike, appear to be one and the same. These citizens cannot believe it is a part of their civic duty to look upon such hatred and suffering. While they stare in disbelief, accompanying testimony makes it hard to breathe.

Eighteen-year-old Michelle Chapman takes the stand. The young woman identifies letters written to her by the defendant from prison. At the time, she was fifteen to seventeen years old. The defense pops up to object. But it is overruled. Three of the nineteen letters Chapman has given to the FBI are introduced as evidence.

A 1996 letter from Beto sounds almost as if King were writing to himself, not this impressionable young girl. He asked, "What do I have to look forward too [sic] returning to Jasper?" In case she had no answer, King provided one: "A town full of race traitoring nigger loveing [sic] whores?" He speculated that maybe the "Jews and niggers will kill one another before long."

King's lawyer hangs his head. Now it is clear why Cribbs makes one objection after another. His client has not even spoken and already King's words make a powerful impact, just as they did when he refused to listen to the advice of his attorney before firing off a rambling seven-page statement to the *Dallas Morning News*.

King shows no visible interest in what Chapman says, but looks pleased to see the pretty girl again, who, in turn, looks terrified to face the author of the jailhouse love letters. She testifies that King also wrote to ask her feelings on minorities: "Would you date one, fuck one and become a race trader [sic] like a lot of those whores in Jasper?"

There is an audible reaction from the courtroom when Chapman testifies that King is most proud of a tattoo "of a black man hanging on his arm." She confirms King's penchant for bragging about his prison tattoos. Chapman is excused.

Tommy Robinson, the veteran investigator with the Jasper County Sheriff's Office, is in the witness box to offer an exclusive perspective on the collection of evidence. His main job at the crime scene was to photograph three miles of evidence cast from one side of the road to the other, and he now has the task of outlining this information for the jury. Then a childhood friend testifies that he saw Byrd at a party; another, Steven Scott, is the state's only eyewitness who can actually place the victim on the back of a step-side truck. The sad crescendo builds.

Witness number six is Mary Verrett, one of the Byrd sisters. Her voice trembles as Verrett testifies that she last saw her brother the day before the murder when family members gathered to decorate for an evening bridal shower about to be given for a niece. Verrett tells the jury that her brother was wearing a San Francisco tourist cap another sister had given him as a gift.

Nervous and ready to battle tears, the poised woman touches personal effects, bagged objects gingerly placed in front of her. "Yes, it is the same watch I gave him." Verrett had joked with her childhood protector that he could keep an inexpensive watch left behind by her husband at Byrd's apartment. (Her husband had two identical watches so she didn't think he would mind parting with one.) It was ripped from Byrd's arm as he was dragged down Huff Creek Road.

An insensitive cross-examination question is useless: "Was any drinking done at the shower?" Verrett answers no and steps down. She walks, with head held high, back to her front-row seat. How she keeps the tears at bay no one can figure.

More defense objections erupt over what investigators want to tell jurors they recovered from King's apartment. Judge Golden will allow the contents of a mysterious folder to be used by the prosecution "in a limited manner."

Ralph Nichols, a Jasper County constable, and Joe Sterling identify items found in the defendant's apartment, incriminating things that seem to validate the prosecution's opening statement that King planned to start his own local chapter of the Texas Rebel Soldiers. There is a plan in King's own handwriting, as well as other racist documents and literature. Investigators testify about a receipt for *The Silent Brotherhood,* a book King has ordered that describes the activities of a well-known group of violent extremists known as the Order. Members gained notoriety in the early 1980s for a string of bombings and other crimes, including the murder of a Denver talk show host.

As testimony concludes on the first day, photographers are warned not to try anything sneaky. No pictures of jurors are allowed. And none of the family. As James Byrd, Sr., and his six daughters file by, respectful journalists do not dare yell at them or scream questions. One very thoughtful reporter from Houston, whom the family has grown to trust, simply asks, "How you holding up?" Never missing a step, one sister looks back. "It's been a very tough day."

After the sickening testimony, few care about dinner. It is the last thing on my mind as I march to the DA's crowded office to request permission to examine the inconceivable. "I need to see the crime scene photos, and I have a right to, as part of my job." Guy James Gray's assistant, Novie Hammock, gives me a second look and seems puzzled at the request. "Are you sure?" It frightens me that her large, pretty eyes get so much bigger. Of course I'm not sure. I respond honestly, "No, but I'm going on. I need to see them."

Not at all happy about my public-information rights to view the photos, she tosses her wavy blond hair and looks at me. "Okay, but it'll take a few minutes because they're upstairs in a vault." I picture some dark, winding staircase that leads to a musty old attic, probably guarded by a pair of hungry rottweilers. While the assistant is gone, I make at least two attempts to leave. My mind definitely says go, but my body resists. I nervously look at my watch. Only seventeen minutes before my next live report.

When I'm not in court or interviewing prosecutors or members of the Byrd family, I am doing around-the-clock reports for Dallas and New York. Lately, given the attention the rest of the world has focused on this case, I find myself in a new position—that of international commentator. Live, on the BBC, a very British voice posed an interesting question: "Miss King, are all the people in Jasper like these three?" I responded with a laugh, "As a native Texan, I know very few people who behave the way these boys have." My commentary also gets prime time play on Ireland Radio, Canadian Radio, and Radio New Zealand, and a host of talk shows in the States. I even find myself in the unenviable position of having to do "live" television, which is terrifyingly unpredictable. All these things work in concert to jump-start what was, as a result of the firing, a dwindling supply of self-esteem. I now find myself eager to believe that I can meet one of the biggest challenges of my life. Though exhaustion will wait for me at the end of each day and I desperately miss my kids, I don't mind the hard work that begins each morning at 4 A.M. and continues until midnight, when I drift off to sleep and all that happened finds its way into my short dreams.

Around the globe come requests from media organizations that want to speak to a journalist who "lives" this case, is deep in the trenches, and can "put others in Jasper," as one producer says to me. Now, as I wait for Novie, I believe that if I see these horrific photos I'll be better prepared to do that. I'll also be able to put myself in the jury box and have more empathy for the people who must decide John William King's fate.

Just as I wonder what takes Novie so long, she appears with those large questioning eyes of hers, as if to say "Still here?" Surrounded by antsy colleagues who all hope to get some nugget on strategy if they hang out and pester prosecutors, Novie leads me to her boss' office. Finally, just above a whisper, she speaks: "Come in here." Without a word, Novie removes a black portfolio from underneath the inside of her jacket. She is uncomfortable.

Gently, Novie lays the black book on the big desk, then looks at me again. She asks, "Are you ready?" I nod. Then the executive assistant to the district attorney gives one stipulation: "Do not touch the book—you must tell me when to turn the page and I will." Tell her? I must verbally request a change in pages, I realize, because she refuses to look.

With only five minutes before my next live report, Novie opens to the first grisly photo of the victim. I look at what is left of James Byrd, Jr., body parts missing, skinned up, broken and barren, void of life. Hand over my mouth, I almost go screaming from the room. I never recover from the shock of the first photo, or any of the others for that matter. I do not know what nightmares these photos will later spawn. I am stunned and speechless.

She has seen them once and does not ever wish to again. I

understand completely. I try my best to sound composed, professional, like the tough-as-nails journalist I'm supposed to be. I brace against no one but myself. Each time I indicate to her I am ready to digest another haunting image of Mr. Byrd, my shaky voice betrays me. I am now where I set out to be—in the jury box.

Although never a death penalty advocate, I am instantly convinced by these photos that punishment in this case must be swift and severe. I am glad I do not have to decide. "Turn the page," I say again. Novie does, with her neck still perched as far to the left as it will go. I cannot make it all the way to the end of the book. "That's enough, thank you," I say. I regret not listening to my husband, a fellow journalist, and other shell-shocked colleagues who saw the photos ahead of me.

I dash out of the Jasper County Courthouse and place my sunglasses over my face to cover the tears racing down my cheeks. I look at my watch—I have less than two minutes before my next scheduled report.

Away from the front door, I move down the sidewalk and step farther into the faded sunlight to compose myself. Ten seconds later, I am on the air live. The horrendous, grotesque pictures flash before my eyes as I speak. I can hardly stay composed for the forty seconds I am on the air. It feels like forever. It is the only time over the span of a twenty-year broadcast career that I almost lose it— live, on the air. I hang up the cell phone and place my hand back over my mouth. The courthouse lawn is packed with inquisitive colleagues. No one knows what is wrong with me. Several people stare. All I can do is cry.

Now I understand what jurors feel when they view 8-by-10-inch color photos of the crime scene. I now have some small clue about the state's strategy to show these devastating photos early, to show them in a private way, so that there is no chance of desensitization.

I understand the necessary apologies made by prosecutors to the jury. More than anything, I understand, and in fact am relieved by, the state's decision not to show these photos in open court with the victim's family present. After all, the Byrds have never seen them. I hope they never will.

Back in court, a Black Muslim makes a rare outburst when he leaps from his seat and storms out. The man in the gold suit, Mister X, talks the entire time he walks. Cameras take aim and reporters give chase to find out what has set him off. Judge Golden lightly bangs the gavel at the agitated man's exit. Even without a microphone, the black man's words ring out. "It will be a travesty of justice if these guys walk . . . all hell will break loose." He is met with a warm response from law enforcement, who later provide a police escort out of town.

On the stand, Keisha Adkins finishes her testimony about the contact she had with the three defendants prior to the murder. Prosecutors are building their time line. Curtis Frame, considered the lead local investigator on the case, testifies extensively about the collection of evidence. Frame describes what he saw on Huff Creek Road—"a very mangled, torn-up torso of a body."

When court is again dismissed, tension and tempers are higher and louder. Hecklers taunt King as he is escorted back to the Jasper County Jail. "Why should he get special treatment?" Several blacks want to know where King's prison stripes are, why he gets to wear street clothes. One onlooker blasts police for their kindly treatment of "a prisoner."

At the news conference Judge Golden has ordered both sides to attend, Cribbs, the lead defense attorney, is asked, "Do King's tattoos make him a racist?" Cribbs, who resembles a dying man unable to successfully complete his last mission in life, quips back, "Is it possible for a bear to be a bear without hair?"

No matter what reporters do or ask, politely or aggressively, Cribbs refuses to publicly confirm his defense strategy. With his cross-examination of select state witnesses comes the insinuation that some pretty tough African-American inmates run the North Side of the Beto unit where King did time. And as a consequence of serving time there, King has become a hard-core white supremacist.

The parade of state witnesses resumes with Jasper Police Detective Rich Ford. Anxious to tear into Ford, defense attorneys begin without the jury present. It brings a roar of laughter when the judge looks at the empty chairs: "Wait, gotta bring in the jury first."

"Do you know what a wood is?" Ford is asked. He defines it as a white person who stands up for himself in prison. A "ho," according to Ford, is an inmate who submits sexually. Interested jurors are told that $60 is all an inmate is allowed every two weeks. Should they decide to "up" that $60, it means extortion money will change hands. More prison lingo is defined. Then Ford admits that tattoos and symbols may be a means of survival, an admission that supports what opposing counsel implies.

Ford's classes on satanic meanings come in handy when defense attorney Brack Jones compares a Baphomet symbol to a "Congressional Medal of Honor." The upside-down pentagram is located on the back of King's head; it is considered among the most potent signs of Satanism and represents the goat's head. Those with military service do not appreciate the desperate comparison. The defense attorney cannot shake Ford from his belief that there is a connection between satanic symbols and racist groups.

Guy James Gray supports what Ford has to say with state exhibits that the defense does not want jurors to examine. Exhibit number 50 shows photos of King with his shirt off. It also high-lights documents that Ford testifies are proof that King wanted to start a local chapter of the Texas Rebel Soldiers. There is a copy of an application for membership in the Confederate Knights of America, their bylaws, a code of ethics, and a "welcome" letter to new members. Twenty-six pages in King's own handwriting are irrefutable. The proposed date for the new chapter's formation: July 4, 1998, almost a full month after the murder of James Byrd, Jr., just enough time to make the killers notorious for such a vicious crime.

Special agents from the Federal Bureau of Investigation con-tribute by sharing a mountain of done-by-the-book evidence, bagged, photographed, and analyzed. Evidence comes from King's apartment, Shawn Berry's truck, Huff Creek Road, as well as clothes and shoes worn by the defendants. A lone drop of blood found on King's brown sandals measured less than a tenth of an inch, but it was enough for tests to show conclusively it was Byrd's blood. Every shred of government evidence is accounted for and shared with the jury. DNA experts testify about other scientific results. Tires from the gray truck are even rolled into the court-room.

Father Ron Foshage, a local priest, enters to comfort King's father, who never gets out of his wheelchair. Instead, he is parked near the front row, directly behind the defense table and the son he loves. King's biological mother could not be persuaded to attend. After stern warnings from her spiritual advisor, the woman who now makes Baton Rouge, Louisiana, her home, refused to offer physical or emotional support to the son she gave away. King's father more than makes up for her permanent absence and even says he understands the explanation that her minister gave—the trial would be far too stressful. That anxiety is keenly felt as testimony goes on and on, some of it tediously deliberate, to lessen any chance for possible appellate victory. Witness number fifteen, however, halts the sleepy proceedings with a personal nightmare.

Twenty-eight-year-old William Hoover provides a grave account of life at Beto. Though he is a state witness, escorted to town by FBI agents, certain things that Hoover admits under defense questioning bolster the case Cribbs and Jones are thought to be building. Hoover testifies that when he resided on the North Side of Beto I, it was 70 percent black. He offers no documentation. Hoover is a former Aryan Brotherhood member who has been out of the gang about fourteen months. When asked about rival gangs, Hoover responds, "The CKA was small in that unit; the Aryan Circle helped them to get started."

Hoover, the son of a police officer and now a full-time college student, further testifies that King talked about initiating a new member who would be required to demonstrate loyalty by torturing and killing a black man. Hoover tells shocked jury members that King spoke of his intention to kidnap a black and put him in the trunk of a car, then "take them out into the woods," a scenario close to what prosecutors charge.

When asked if King had the same feelings about Jewish people, Hoover responds, "He concentrated on the Jews more than the other races." Many of the reporters, myself included, interview a number of people who express mild surprise that King's ravenous hatred extends beyond the black race. Hoover confirms that King seriously believed, or hoped, there would someday be a race war between blacks and whites, or whites and Jews. Before he leaves the stand, Hoover makes it plain he did not want to testify and fears for his own safety. "I was told it was mandatory to be here."

Hoover is adamant that soon after King got to "the pen" he had to make a choice about whether he was going to be a "wood or a ho." King chose to be a wood, a person who stands for the white race. The Hoover demonstration is effective for both sides, but still does not evoke enough collective sympathy to override what King is accused of.

During the break, a spectator reminds all, "The state of Texas is not on trial." That does not stop Sonny Cribbs from trying to make the Texas Department of Criminal Justice an accomplice.

A changing parade of FBI agents, local investigators, and other witnesses take the stand. They all have a job to do. None do it quite like Dr. Tommy Brown, the forensic pathologist.

He delivers a crushing legal blow, the most damning evidence of all. Voice smooth and steady, Brown wallops the jury by slowly and methodically describing detailed injuries suffered by the victim.

During Dr. Brown's riveting testimony, many are moved by the absolutely calm manner in which the expert delivers the results of his autopsy on Byrd. Shaken jurors visualize the torn-up body of James Byrd, Jr. The left cheekbone is completely exposed and dentures are "absent," according to Dr. Brown. Silence gives way to uncomfortable squirms. There is a 7-inch gash, a 5½-inch contusion, "skin-deep" abrasions and "severe lacerations," cuts and bruises all over. Jurors don't want the details, but it is a part of their job to listen to a journey of pain.

Dr. Brown never once changes the tranquilizing tone of his voice. He is compassionately monotonic and brings a sense of authority to the case. Some family members excuse themselves from the courtroom. Surprisingly, some stay, and that prompts an even higher degree of respect from the media. By the looks on their anguished faces, they pray the agonizing testimony will soon be over. Dr. Brown continues up Huff Creek Road.

As the seasoned pathologist explains the dramatic differences between pre- and postmortem colors, he tells the jury, "Mr. Byrd was conscious and was attempting to relieve some of the pain while being dragged." Jurors are asked to turn in their photo books to a picture of the back of the victim's head while Dr. Brown convinces them that "Mr. Byrd was alive just before his head was severed." Once again, the words "alive and conscious" reverberate like the sound of giant orchestral cymbals.

As Dr. Brown's hour-long testimony comes to an end, jury members try hard not to show emotion. Several exhausted reporters take loud deep breaths with a sense of collective relief that the end is near. When the good doctor steps down, excitement builds and everyone is braced for the state to rest. After Dr. Brown's powerful testimony, there doesn't appear to be much more the state can add to its already compelling case.

Before anxious jurors can begin to digest three miles of pain, or the family can recover from the long list of injuries, lights are dimmed slightly and the state prepares to present one final witness. But it is not a witness at all. Thanks to technology and a homemade video projected onto a white screen, reporters inside the courtroom, civilians, prosecutors, the defense, and the victim's family are about to take a journey on the road traveled that night by the murderers. Dr. Brown's final comments segue dramatically into the start of the silent video. The crowded room has such perfect quiet, solemnity, and stillness, to make a sound would be a sign of disrespect.

The gritty homemade tape, magnified on a simple classroom projection screen, enables every person in the courtroom to get behind the wheel, factor in all the turns and all the stops taken by King, Brewer, and Berry. The video details the drive down Huff Creek Road, some of the three-mile journey of green trees, shrubs, and blue sky. And then there are things that jurors had not heard about: homes, landmarks, and rusty mailboxes. Each one can hear the metallic clangor of a 24½-foot chain wrapped around the substitute vehicle in the video.

In one portion of the silent video, the driver pauses, uncomfortably long, at the concrete culvert where James Byrd, Jr., was decapitated. The silence is penetrating and does not end until the video comes to one of the oldest black cemeteries in the county, where the fragmented body was released from the chain.

As the eleven-minute video fades, then finally ends, Guy James Gray proudly stands in the quiet, half-dark room to face Judge Joe Bob Golden. After presenting more than forty witnesses, the State of Texas rests.

Assistant District Attorney Pat Hardy once described defense attorney Sonny Cribbs as "Dirty Harry" because the Beaumont-based lawyer takes all the grimy capital cases nobody else will touch.

Staunchly opposed to the death penalty, Cribbs opens his defense by giving jurors another taste of the racial climate he believes is a mitigating factor that shaped the views of John William King. It is time to meet the still incarcerated Beto inmate who painted some of King's tattoos.

Six feet three inches tall, and weighing more than 270 pounds, John "Big Mo" Mosley enters the courtroom under heavy security. Instantly, discomfort blankets the courtroom. Bald, muscular, and the epitome of tough, Mosley makes it known immediately that he does not suffer fools or abuse behind bars: "If you don't fight, you have to give 'em your mama's money, and sexual favors."

Mosley tells jurors that some people do get certain tattoos for protection. "Ain't too many people going to ask for butterflies and roses." Under any other circumstance, the comment might produce laughter. But the Beto inmate is more scary than he is funny.

As prosecutors prepare to question Mosley, he turns and winks at King. Then the intimidator admits he "sent word" to another inmate who was set to testify against the defendant that a change of heart would go a long way in the self-preservation department. The incentive from Mosley apparently worked. In contrast, there were other witnesses, according to Cribbs, who reneged on agreements to join Mosley and provide defense testimony. A black inmate from Beto made it all the way to Jasper, where he was interviewed for trial. Cribbs tells me his appearance would've included his testimony that he had no problems with King and that the two were friendly, even occasionally sharing the same cigarette. Cribbs hints that the black man got cold feet; a talk with his father convinced him not to get involved. Cribbs suspects a talk with the FBI also went a long way to change the scared inmate's mind.

The jury will also never get to hear from an inmate who penned a letter to the *Dallas Morning News* in 1998 to say that he could understand why King might have committed this crime. Nor can Cribbs bemoan the fact that life in prison would be tough for any inmate who testifies for King, with the possible exception of Mosley, whose badass reputation ensures his safety.

After a former roommate and employer also testify, the defense rests. Their entire case takes one hour to present. John William King does not take the stand. Cribbs looks disappointed and defeated.

It is ten-fifteen on Tuesday morning, February 23, 1999, time for closing arguments. Pat Hardy politely thanks the jury, then reminds them, "On the 7th day of June 1998, James Byrd, Jr., was murdered and that's the bottom line." His throaty voice rises when he is passionate or angry about something, so much so that he cannot even hear the feverish pitch as it climbs. "It's obvious the man was drug to death behind a motor vehicle," Hardy starts, then continues in the infamous Southern drawl, "The state has proven its case beyond a reasonable doubt."

Several of Hardy's facial expressions lend fire to his close. "If you look at the evidence, you'll see what Mr. King and his cohorts thought of black people." Hardy shakes his head as if to wave off the defendants in total disrespect, then tells the jury that it took three much younger men to handle a half-intoxicated forty-nine-year-old black man. "Where's the honor in that?" Hardy shrugs.

His close is short, eloquent, and fiery; it touches on all the highlights from the trial—the tattoos, the victim, the defense that King drastically changed after prison, his codefendants, and the vicious murder itself. Smart and furious, Hardy turns, looks in King's direction, stares back at the jury, and tells them Byrd was killed by "three robed riders coming straight out of hell. Instead of a rope, they used a chain. Instead of a horse, they used a pickup."

Pat Hardy sits down. When he used his powerful "three robed riders" analogy, I could relate. What is barely fathomable is the unlikely source of these words—a Southern-raised, middle-aged white man with a gun and a badge. It is a stand against racial violence, the kind few people who look like him ever make in places like East Texas.

When Sonny Cribbs delivers closing arguments, it is clear the death penalty opponent is striving for one goal—to save King's life. Cribbs doesn't deny that King was at the scene of the crime, but he does argue against any notion of premeditation. Cribbs' entire defense is based on what happened to King during his stint in the Texas Department of Criminal Justice. Cribbs compares the psychological effects of prison to some kind of posttraumatic syndrome that bedevils a lot of war veterans. "This boy had something happen to him in the pen. He became a racist. He became a hater, but that's his right." Cribbs lukewarmly defends his client, then adds, "If you feel the State of Texas has not proven this case beyond a reasonable doubt, then you must find him not guilty."

Deliberations last only two-and-a-half hours. Jury members vote the lone African-American on the panel, Joe Collins, its foreman. It is Collins, himself a stout corrections officer, who hands the signed verdict form to a bailiff. John William King is found guilty of capital murder. After staring down jurors, King stares straight ahead. Judge Golden issues a warning when spectators show their approval with light applause. King's sister, Carol Spadaccini, dashes into the courtroom and collapses in her father's arms as both openly weep.

Blacks all over East Texas applaud the historic decision. One resident emphatically states, "It wasn't that long ago that a twenty-four-year-old white man would've never been brought to justice for a racially motivated crime." Collins is the same age as the defendant, twenty-four years old, and actually remembers King from school days. But Bill is not the same boy Joe knew in the eighth grade.

Tired from sleepless nights, hours of racist testimony, and the grim knowledge of what lies ahead, jurors prepare for a quick penalty phase and the final decision they are required to make. Should John William King live or die for dragging James Byrd, Jr., to death?

Both sides call professionals to the stand to testify whether King is a future danger, even if granted life in prison. A psychiatrist for the state vociferously argues that King may pose a threat to African-American inmates and is likely to assault other black people if he gets a life sentence and becomes a part of the general prison population.

Defense attorneys counter with a clinical psychologist who tells the jury a life sentence would automatically mean King can be paroled in forty years, something that might lessen the chance for more violence since he would be sixty-four years old. Though the doctor calls violent crime at this age "very unlikely," under cross-examination, the former state prison employee makes an admission that does more for prosecutors than for the defense: "King is a real and viable threat."

When asked if putting King to death is the only way to ensure he will never harm again, the doctor simply nods and says, "True," then adds, "King is a danger to any black or Jew he might have future contact with." A hush falls over the courtroom as everyone looks over to check defense reaction. After all, the doctor is their witness.

Finally, the expert agrees that King expressed no remorse for the dragging murder in a so-called statement made in a jailhouse note to Brewer, a letter confiscated by authorities. It does not help that the defendant appears to doze through much of the debate on whether he is a future danger and on mitigating factors, like prison. Reporters point and whisper. Some snicker.

Ronald King is the second and final penalty-phase witness for the defense. Before his father is wheeled in front of Judge Golden, King, virtually indifferent until now, asks to be removed. He does not want to hear his father beg. King gets his wish and is escorted out.

In the final exchange, the elder King is asked if he loves his son. "Yeah, I love him, but you don't love the things they do." He looks up straight at the judge, says "I don't want him to die," and breaks down beyond control. "Anything's better than losing him." A lot of people cry along with the defendant's sickly father, who is too upset to remain in the courtroom. His daughter wheels him out into the hall. John William King returns to the courtroom, his hard eyes moist and red from what one can only assume is a losing battle to fight back tears. It is the only visible emotion King shows. It is soon confirmed that while King was in the small room authorities placed him in, he could hear every word his father said.

The elder King, frail and dressed in a shabby short-sleeve shirt in the cool of winter, feels an extended arm. Away from the intrusive click of cameras, twenty-eight-year-old Renee Mullins, the oldest daughter of James Byrd, Jr., reaches over to hug Ronald King, who gratefully responds, "Oh God. Thank you." Mullins follows the gesture with another—a long embrace with his daughter. Finally, one of Byrd's six sisters, Betty Boatner, offers more comfort: "He's in God's hands now."

Defense attorneys provide only two witnesses in the penalty phase, and the case goes straight to the jury. Less than three hours after they start to deliberate punishment, jurors reach their final decision. As with his capital murder conviction, King shows no emotion when he is sentenced to die. Judge Golden looks toward the defendant, and then says in a matter-of-fact tone, "I hereby sentence you to death by lethal injection." He pauses. "Sheriff, you may take him to the Department of Criminal Justice to await an execution date."

Unrepentant, the white supremacist looks straight ahead, contumacious to the bitter end. In the damning and prophetic kite (jailhouse note) that comes back to haunt him, King wrote to Brewer, after their arrests, "Regardless of the outcome of this, we have made history and shall die proudly remembered if need be." He gets his wish. King is the first white man sent to Texas' death row for the murder of a black man in almost 150 years, since Reconstruction. If King is executed, he will become the first white Texan put to death for the murder of a black person since 1854, when James "Rhode" Wilson intended to kill a white farmer with whom he had a disagreement but instead killed the man's prize male slave.

Shortly after King's punishment is announced, I file the following network report:

> John William King has been sentenced to death. The King jury deliberated less than three hours after closing arguments. During deliberations, they sent out notes asking to see the homemade shank King fashioned in prison and the letter he wrote to a teenage girl from prison. They also wanted to see the 'kite,' which is the jailhouse note passed between King and codefendant Russell Brewer. After that, the seven-man, five-woman jury emerged with a decision that King must die for dragging James Byrd, Jr., to death. When King was brought out for the last time for his trip to death row, he mouthed an obscenity to the Byrd family. They say that's exactly what they would expect from a man with no remorse. Joyce King, CBS News, Jasper, Texas.

Twenty-four hours later, King, in an ironic twist of fate, is processed for death row at the James Byrd Diagnostic Unit. First, Collins, a black man with whom King attended middle school, is made jury foreman at his trial. And now a facility that bears the very name of his victim is his next stop before being readied for death row. Though the unit is indeed named for James Byrd, it is not the victim, but another James Byrd, who was a warden for the state prison system.

A friend of King's testified that King once told him, "Everywhere we go, it's getting dark," a thinly disguised reference to black people. King could not even stand to see or be around blacks. It's sure to be incredibly dark at his new home.

SEVEN

As the April 19 anniversary of both the Branch Davidian fire near Waco and the Oklahoma City bombing nears, Texas prison officials warn prosecutors that they have intercepted letters from a racist prison gang that hint at some kind of "family reunion" on that date in Jasper.

Guy James Gray tells the media that though the letters don't allude to any violence, the alleged correspondence involves members of the Aryan Circle, one of the eleven security risk groups behind bars. Also, there are references to King and Brewer and something about a tractor pull, and the word "dragging" was mentioned. It is the same Aryan Circle a witness at King's trial credited with helping the Confederate Knights of America get established. An FBI investigation is launched and security is stepped up.

April 19 is a day most Americans remember for two tragedies that will forever be linked. First, in 1993, dozens of Branch Davidians who followed the teachings of cult leader David Koresh died in a fire at their compound. Disgust with the way federal officials handled the preceding fifty-one-day standoff is in turn cited as a motivating factor for the 1995 Oklahoma City bombing in which 168 Americans were killed. No one in Jasper can afford to dismiss coded letters associated in any way with April 19.

To avoid even the appearance of disrespect for the solemn anniversary, a pretrial hearing for Lawrence Russell Brewer is moved from April 19 to April 20. Not long after, Brewer's May trial date is scratched. Instead of presenting opening statements for the second dragging trial in Jasper, Gray fights a change-of-venue motion, which is denied. But then prosecutors decide the best thing might actually be to get the hell out of Dodge, where things are still smoking from what Brewer's attorney charges is the town's "vested interest" in the case.

Gray enlists his good friend Sheriff Billy Rowles to help find a county willing and able to offer Jasper available court space on its docket. The sales pitch takes a toll on both men; they visit six counties with no luck. Twice that many flat out say no on the phone, no trip required. Some of the reasons sound like legitimate excuses. A few community leaders tell Jasper officials they fear old "racial wounds" might be reopened. With the summer tourist season about to begin, a few fear economic ramifications that might result from such a racially explosive capital murder trial.

When it is least expected, one Texas county bravely offers Jasper some assistance.

Officials at the Brazos County Courthouse snap my picture for media credentials. Metal detectors at the sagging courthouse in Bryan, Texas, 150 miles from Jasper, are a sobering reminder that this is serious business. The atmosphere elsewhere in the county does not bear that out.

On a warm, Sunday afternoon, I exhale, wipe my brow, and check into the TownPlace Suites, an extended-stay, furnished room that resembles a small apartment. Its College Station location on University Drive puts me right in the heart of Aggieland, with its 40,000 screaming students at Texas A&M University.

Shockingly relaxed in comparison to Jasper, extracurricular activities are much in evidence with students expressing pride in their cherished maroon and white with "Beat Tulsa" cheers and signs.

The first football game of the season is slated for Saturday. The cheerful, carefree mentality is disturbing. "What trial?" an Aggie responds when I ask his impression of all the hoopla that surrounds the media's extended tour of duty.

I am back at the courthouse at 9 A.M. on Monday, September 13, 1999. Judge Monte Lawlis walks in to call the courtroom to order. Lawrence Russell Brewer calmly sits down and prepares to face the seven men and five women who will hear this case. Though roughly 12 percent of the population in Brazos County is African American, there is not one black on the jury. Ages of the eleven whites and one Hispanic range from twenty-nine to sixty-nine. They listen thoughtfully to instructions and appear relieved at the first Lawlis decision: "For now, you will not be sequestered."

Jasper County District Attorney Guy James Gray opens for the state with a promise to show that all three defendants are active participants in the dragging. "It's not illegal to hate someone, have tattoos, or even preach hatred," Gray starts, "but it is illegal to use acts of racial violence against someone."

The forty-nine-year-old chief prosecutor apologizes to the jury for abominable language they will hear in the trial, especially the word "nigger." Fresh from a few months off and a more stabilized blood pressure, the invigorated DA is ready. Gray tells the panel that Brewer was King's mentor in prison and that Brewer rose as high as someone from the infamous Beto I Unit can in the Confederate Knights of America. Gray starts the long process of prison education for this class of jurors when he mocks the words Brewer allegedly used to begin King's tutelage: "I will school your young ass." Gray cautiously reveals that horrific crime scene photos that the jury will see have never been seen by the public or by the family in open court. "This case belongs to all of us simply because of motive"—Gray pulls the jury closer. "Brewer has written how he sees himself: a hero, a star, a person who has accomplished something with this murder."

What prosecutors hope to accomplish is the foundation for a capital conviction. They can only do that if jurors are satisfied that the legal definition of kidnapping applies to how Byrd's movement was restricted: by chaining his ankles. The second thing the state must secure for a capital conviction is the belief that James Byrd, Jr., was alive when he was chained and dragged. For its first witness, the state calls Sheriff Billy Rowles.

Filled with a sense of déjà vu, I notice Rowles is not wearing his customary dungarees and cropped cowboy jacket, but a maroon sport coat that makes him look more like the father of an Aggie student than the sheriff of Jasper County. Indeed, the maroon conjures up images of the last trip here to see my Aggie husband inducted into the Texas A&M University Hall of Fame. The rich burgundy color, like the jacket I stare at, was everywhere that wonderful day at Kyle Field.

Rowles begins with a description of what he found on Huff Creek Road, details that returning veterans from the first trial do not want to hear a second time. While he talks, fourteen copies of crime scene photo booklets are passed to twelve jurors and two alternates. They stare an incredibly long time with an enormous amount of restraint. As they study the photos, Rowles continues: "Drag marks visible on the nose, elbows ground down, no marks on the back of the head." Troubled expressions form on the faces of several jurors, who now drop their guard. They are misty-eyed, like drained members of the family who sit quietly behind Jasper County prosecutors.

As jurors stare at photos, spectators stare at Brewer. Even with a thirty-pound weight gain, his dapper navy suit is much too large, the sleeves hanging well past his wrists, almost to his knuckles.

These are not his nice clothes at all. It appears that Brewer is wearing another man's clothes the same way he is accused of taking another man's life—very casually.

Brewer's position of Exalted Cyclops is considered one of leadership in the CKA. Like King, Brewer was an avid writer. In a damning, eight-page letter intercepted by jail authorities, Brewer wrote, "Ha! Well I did it; and no longer am I a virgin! It was a rush."

In the same confiscated letter, Brewer wrote that he was "licking" his lips at the deed and wanted more. Sergeant William Kirk, a gang intelligence officer at Beto, testifies that a "tire," which Brewer alluded to in the letter, is a black person, while "roll a tire" means "to assault a black person." Kirk admits the words sound frighteningly close to a confession of a crime against someone black. The defense, in contrast, tries to imply sexual innuendo: "Was the writer saying he's had oral sex for the first time?" Kirk answers no.

Witness number seven is a former Hispanic inmate named Jesus Moran. Once a member of the Texas Syndicate, Moran fearlessly testifies that a cocky, unrepentant Brewer confided in him after the murder: "If he could get away with it completely, he would take the whole black population and shoot them behind the head."

The very next witness is a former CKA member who was housed at Beto in 1995, the same time King and Brewer were there. Mark Postell acknowledges it was "pretty stupid" for Brewer to write that kind of letter to another inmate. Postell tries to convince the jury that he's now ashamed of things done in the name of racism; a personal situation forced him to change. When Postell's young child was diagnosed with leukemia, he got a bone marrow transplant from a black woman that saved the child's life. Postell says he still has hatred for some blacks but not the entire race. Before he is dismissed, Postell makes an estimate about the racial breakdown on Beto's North Side: "It's dangerous to wear a CKA patch in a unit that's eighty percent black."

In contrast to Cribbs' strategy in the King trial, defense attorneys Doug Barlow and Layne Walker fight valiantly to save Brewer and bombard the jury with an overwhelming amount of information. Their client wants to live and does not appear remotely interested in fulfilling the self-proclaimed role of "hero." Defense attorneys methodically pick apart every detail the state provides, twisting the obvious with repetitious statements and commendable attempts to make Brewer seem a somehow salvageable individual. While the state contends he was King's mentor, they paint him as gullible and easily led.

The capable tag team go after timid twenty-two-year-old Keisha Adkins, who is back for a second round. King's former girlfriend, visibly pregnant at the first trial, is now the new mother of a three-month-old, which prompts a loud count backward and questions about the baby's father. Adkins says it is not King. But what else would she say?

More nervous this time, the young woman points out Brewer as the person she remembers from King's apartment just hours before the murder: "Yes, that's him, but he had more tattoos." They are still there underneath someone else's oversized suit.

Adkins does remarkably well for a self-conscious young woman with low self-esteem, a new baby, and frayed nerves. But she gets hammered by defense attorneys who repeatedly ask about the motivation for going to King's apartment on June 6, 1998. At one point, the young woman, so flustered and ashamed, looks up at

Judge Lawlis: "Do I have to answer that?" After she can take no more, Adkins, with tears in her eyes, humiliated, finally answers, "I was in the bedroom with Bill." Still not satisfied, Brewer's lawyers force her to respond to a direct question about whether or not they were engaged in sexual activity. Hoping for rescue, Adkins looks longingly in the prosecutors' direction, hesitates, then utters a very low, very slow, muffled "Yes."

Barlow and Walker try to paint Adkins as a frightened little sex toy, too dumb to see that she's testifying against their client because of her undying allegiance to King. Through the rough ride, Adkins hangs on, desperately clinging to her position that she had no prior knowledge of any plan to commit a crime. She again testifies that King showed her the tattoo of a black man hanging, as well as a few others. Still, woefully ignorant or willingly indifferent, Adkins maintains that she doesn't think King's tattoos mean anything.

Another state witness treated to the sneak-up-and-clobber tactic is veteran investigator Tommy Robinson. As he squirms in the witness seat, Barlow and Walker fire a barrage of questions about whether gloves used at the crime scene needed to be changed to collect every piece of evidence. It is a blatant suggestion to the jury that the investigation was tainted by a bunch of hick Keystone Kops.

Brewer's relentless duo grill Robinson about his training. "Would you agree with me that you were in way over your head?" Robinson resents the question. Red-faced, he spits out a one-word response: "No." He is on the stand for two hours to defend the collection of sensitive evidence. The dirty legal legerdemain goes on, and the Beaumont-based attorneys put up an exceptional fight to deliver Brewer from death row.

Several returning witnesses take the stand, including Billy Mahathay, Steven Scott, Mary Verrett, and Jasper Police Detective

Rich Ford, who, with his vast knowledge of tattoos, what they mean, and why someone chooses to wear certain types, is mesmerizing. Ford explains the elements that make up the CKA patch: a burning cross, a Confederate flag, Klan symbols, a swastika, and more. Jurors learn of words found on white arms, backs, and torsos—words like "peckerwood," "100 percent loco wood" (crazy white person)—then see images of a black man hanging, lightning bolts, and warrior creeds that include "Death Before Dishonor," which is located on Brewer's body.

Defense attorneys try to discount some of Ford's definitions, especially the initials F.T.W., which are scrawled on Brewer's body. Ford is not comfortable repeating what it stands for in mixed company: "'Fuck the World' or 'Fuck the Warden.'" Unhappy with the brash and cavalier attitude the initials suggest of their client, defense attorneys attempt to prove it's an old Harley saying, "Forever Two Wheels," which provokes light, uneasy laughter. Doug Barlow stares down the big detective with one question: "Are people who ride Harleys all racist killers?" Ford politely answers, "No sir." Ford's concession that some whites in prison actually do get tattoos for protection marks a minor advance for the defense. It is followed by another sensible admission that not all people who hate minorities turn out to be killers.

For the tattoo segment, there is a surprise on Brewer's body—a drawing of a family friend from church, a woman the defendant greatly admires. There are no racist connotations. Another drawing is that of a man with a noose around his neck.

Twenty-six-year-old Tommy Faulk is the lead-off prosecution witness on Thursday, September 16. Faulk confirms that he gave consent on Monday, June 8, 1998, for agents to search his property. Then Faulk tries hard to convince this jury, just as he did the authorities, that he didn't know the chain was buried in his yard.

Barlow and Walker get the state witness to admit what he does know: that their client was never actually seen with the chain and didn't know where it was buried. FBI Agent Norm Townsend is back to repeat his role in Jasper. He and other agents escorted Shawn Berry to Faulk's house; it was Berry who directed them behind the house to what Townsend describes as a "depression in the ground." Underneath a board, in dark concealment, was the log chain.

Anticipation drapes the entire courtroom. Pat Hardy, who conducts this critical portion of the state's case, reaches into a secret box to begin the enormous extension task. As Townsend comes down from the witness stand to help the assistant DA, he confirms it is indeed the same rusty 24½-foot-long chain taken from Faulk's yard.

As Hardy unwraps the heavy chain, each thud is more unnerving than the last. This chain—or any other for that matter—is what another Byrd sister, Clara Taylor, calls "symbolic of what her ancestors went through." After Hardy extends the entire chain, which takes a painful eternity, he holds it up high, so each juror can get a good long look. Several people look away; a couple of jurors, some with tears in their eyes, put their face in their hands. Some lean forward, as if to brace some anticipated fall. The obvious discomfort torments Betty Boatner, perhaps the most emotional of all the Byrd sisters. She gets up from her front-row seat and opts for the very last row, along the courtroom wall. She dabs at tears and eventually confesses, "It is all too much."

To unravel it completely, Hardy has to walk right by Brewer, seated at the defense table on the opposite side of the room. As

Hardy stands at the far wall, Brewer's face turns white as a ghost. In an unnatural position, Brewer looks straight ahead, not daring to turn to the side, look away, or look at that chain. Any movement might remind a hostile jury that this is the same man who sarcastically wrote, "What's the worst they can possibly do? Pull prints off a twenty-foot rusty ass log chain?"

Brewer stares at his lawyer's computer screen while agent Barrett A. Mills testifies that he initialed the chain and ran lab tests for stain patterns. Mills explains how he took measurements to determine that the chain now being viewed is the exact same kind that made an indelible impression in the bed of the gray truck. There is also testimony that King and Byrd have DNA on the same crime scene cigarette, which leave theorists to suggest that the white supremacist lit up, then granted his victim one last drag before things went ballistic.

By afternoon recess, more than forty witnesses have come and gone. None make as dramatic and lasting an impression as one key piece of evidence—the log chain.

His nickname is Spiderman. As a trusty in the Jasper County Jail in June and July of 1998, Curtis Johnson was allowed to mow the lawn, tend the garden, and work inside. Johnson testifies that he was given three kites by Brewer to be taken to King when both were jailed after the crime. The diesel mechanic says he assumed the role of go-between when King first asked him to carry something to Brewer and wait for a response. Asked if he is promised any benefits for his testimony, Johnson wants the jury to understand his role of messenger-turned-informant: "The dragging just wasn't right."

Portions of the kites are read in open court; they come across as being written by two people who knew the jig was up. Among those shared aloud: "I lived hard, I'm going to die young, I'm damn sure going to leave a beautiful memory." There is also a braggart tone: "Look at O.J., we are bigger stars, or should I say hero of the day? A life sentence would do us no justice." On cross-examination, one of Brewer's lawyers tries to suggest that some of the jailhouse notes passed between his client and King were simply lyrics borrowed from a rock group.

As Curtis leaves the stand, out in the hall Dr. Tommy Brown hears his name and enters through the rear courtroom doors. Before Judge Lawlis allows the Jefferson County medical examiner inside, Lawlis pauses, out of consideration for the family, to grant permission to leave to anyone who needs to do so. Betty Boatner returns to the back of the room.

As instructed, jurors slowly follow along in the black photo books, accompanied by Dr. Brown's long list of injuries. The family sits quietly. They comfort each other through the brunt of Brown's lengthy testimony, some with arms folded, afraid to blink, afraid to move lest they break down completely. "Skin scraped off, broken back, knees ground down flat, joints and ligaments exposed"—Brown guides the jury over the same nightmarish photos I now find impossible to erase from my mind. Darrell Verrett, the victim's handsome nephew, slumps down in his seat. Just as he does, I hear the words "Toes missing."

Brewer stares straight ahead; he does not look over at the jury, the doctor, or the Byrd family. There is heavy breathing all throughout the courtroom—from the media section, the prosecution's table, the jury box, even up high on the bench. Although all are ready for Brown to stop the torture, he continues, "The penis is shredded and testicles removed by the dragging." The forensic pathologist is adamant that Byrd was alive and conscious and in devastating pain when he managed a commendable struggle to use his knees and elbows to "alleviate the pain."

As Norm Townsend returns to the stand, Betty Boatner makes her way back to the front of the courtroom. Townsend confirms he ordered a video of Huff Creek Road and now enters it as the State's exhibit number 116. Evidence circles, relatively clear, round, and faded, mark the points in the road where pieces of a life were found. The victim's sister, Mary Verrett, calmly wipes away tears.

During the eleven-minute silent ride, someone in the darkened room whispers, "Look at Brewer." I squint to capture his reaction. As Brewer intently watches the video, he perspires profusely. His pudgy wet face never turns from the screen.

The state rests at five-fifteen, and I dart out to the second-floor ladies room and my regular stall, where I now throw up daily.

Lead defense attorney Doug Barlow points his body toward the jury. "You've heard lots of evidence, but very little about who did what." Then, in thespian fashion, Barlow sympathetically looks at his client, pauses, and finally looks back at the jury. "Russell was out there on that logging road, but you don't know who did what." Barlow continues, more convincingly: "It's taken a year to get to know this man. You'll find out Russell is not a killer."

Terry Pelz, the criminal justice consultant, totally disagrees with the state's assertion that Brewer's letter about rolling a tire reads like a confession. The former assistant warden believes code language used in the correspondence represents nothing more than one inmate bragging to another about a sexual act he has performed for the first time, on a woman. Hence the reference to Brewer no longer being "a virgin."

Pelz explains that prison has its own slang and that inmates utilize the jargon to look tough with lies about participation in things they have never done. He says Brewer fits the profile of "talking the talk, not walking the walk." Before Pelz wraps up his ninety minutes on the stand, he offers an opinion on the first defendant. "There is no doubt in my mind that John William King was the one who attempted to control things." According to Pelz, King kept Brewer in the dark about several things, including a letter he wrote to William Hoover expressing an interest in joining the Aryan Brotherhood.

After a twenty-minute recess, Lawrence Russell Brewer is the second and final witness defense attorneys call. The high school dropout looks pained, waives his right not to testify, and begins to answer simple questions about his background, education, criminal record, and when he first became enamored with tattoos. Slow to answer and easy to frustrate, Brewer comes across as a modern day tenderfoot sniffing around the jury for sympathy for the mishaps in his life.

Brewer's voice cracks as he talks about his home away from home, the infamous East Texas prison unit some reporters now jokingly refer to as "Black Beto." Brewer sniffles and tries to make the jury understand exactly how inmates are sized up. "I didn't know what was going on. All the new guys have to be checked." Brewer is quick to explain that everyone at Beto had tattoos all over their arms (full-sleeve) and back and that to walk around without them was merely an invitation for trouble. He wipes at his burning face. "Whenever they get through sexually abusing you, then they trade you for favors. You are considered their property."

Brewer continues to groan and tell horror stories about prison life and how he stood up for himself by staring down any potential confrontations without a fight or scratch. In one breath, he complains about the severity of getting checked and fears that he'd be used as sexual bait, but in the next he expects jurors to believe that, at 5 feet 6 and 145 pounds or so, larger, tougher inmates mostly left him alone.

Brewer testifies that he was immediately approached by the CKA and offered protection under the umbrella of membership. Brewer was the third person to join the Confederate Knights of America, a newly established group that he became a part of "on the spot." Brewer says he didn't want to be a sitting target in prison. "Yes sir, I cut my left thumb, with a razor blade, wiped it on my right thumb, and signed."

Eventually, Brewer met King in prison. They knew each other about six or seven months, before King was released. "He was way ahead of me as far as his vocabulary, his ideas and thoughts," Brewer explains. Defense attorneys consistently push their thesis that Brewer was not the great mastermind of this crime, nor was he smart enough to convince others to follow him. Brewer confirms his admiration for King and how anxious he was to hook up with him again.

While waiting for his release Brewer recalls a time when his mother brought to the prison the son he had fathered with Sylvia Nunes. "I didn't want other people to see me with him. They would ask me whose kid that was." Brewer appears to break down. His face is crinkled, still pained, and crocodile tears remain on the edge of his eyes. "I didn't want them to hurt me," he continues. His unbridled shame at fathering a half-Hispanic child does not go over well with the jury, all white except for one Hispanic. At the same time, many of them look confused, perhaps wondering what kind of white supremacist would marry a Hispanic woman in the first place. So it gives weight to the defense notion that Brewer developed his violent, racist persona to survive prison. The focus then turns to John William King.

Brewer initiated contact with King, outside of prison, first in late 1997, then again in March of 1998. King invited Brewer to Jasper; he bought a bus ticket in April. Brewer suddenly pushes the microphone away and starts to sniffle even louder. This time, there are real tears. He seems torn up about King, a man he respects, looks up to, and now a man he knows will be angry at this public account.

Testimony continues when Brewer angrily denies that he ever told a fellow inmate that he wanted to shoot all black people in the head. "I'm not the smartest guy in the world, but why would I tell a Hispanic person that?" Brewer does confess to using the word "spearchucker," but only to quote Shawn Berry. He also admits that he used "nigger" a handful of times in letters and is not proud that he has referred to black people as "the Tobys," a reference to *Roots* and the slave name given to Kunte Kinte. Some laugh, but only as if to dismiss him completely, when they discover how Brewer spells a written racial epithet: "n-i-g-e-r."

Even the judge finds it hard to follow his own rules about displaying emotion. Lawlis looks disgusted. At noon, he bangs the gavel and adjourns the session for lunch.

Brewer's time on the stand is well defined by Walker and Barlow. They want to show a remorseful, likable person who has more of a child's personality than an adult's. It is Layne Walker who superbly guides Brewer the last step of the way.

There is more specious elucidation, more odd stories about stolen meat and beer runs, stories about oral sex and "featherwoods," a prison term for white females. Then Brewer comes to the eagerly anticipated part of his story. By now, the details are known by heart. It is Saturday night, June 6, 1998, when Keisha Adkins arrived at the Timbers Apartments.

Most of what he says perfectly matches Adkins' testimony, except Brewer claims that Berry was drunk. Brewer corroborates the dragging of a wooden mailbox, an activity that broke strict rules for his parole, as did his association with King. Not long after the mailbox, the trio came across James Byrd, Jr., on the side of the road.

According to Brewer, King issued a dire warning not to pick him up, but Berry ignored it and pulled over. He acknowledges a stop at BJ's to use the bathroom, but then Brewer's testimony begins to shift. He says Berry visited more with Byrd, a man Brewer had never seen before in his life, one who suddenly asked to "ride in the front."

King was so angered by the black man's presence that he told Berry the only way he'd get back in the truck was if Berry agreed to take Byrd straight home. Another stop (and another chance to let Byrd out of the truck), if jurors believe Brewer's version, was made at King's apartment so the men could put on sweaters for the ride. Anyone familiar with Texas weather knows that June, even at night, on the back of a truck, is not particularly cool. Brewer says King wanted everyone to see how mad he was. "At that point, that's all I know—we're taking Byrd home." The victim's family glare at the defendant, not believing the circumspect tale he continues to weave.

Approximately twenty minutes after Byrd was picked up, the four men were on the logging road. Brewer has unwittingly placed King at the crime scene; the convicted man has adamantly denied to authorities he was ever present. Brewer begins to sweat, knowing what he says next will either save him from the death house or help put the needle in his arm. Oldest of the three, the now thirty-two-year-old man didn't know where he was, so he asked King, "Where the hell are we going?" King told Brewer it was Shawn's daddy's land, to which Brewer informs the jury he didn't think anyone lived in woods that thick. "It didn't even look like a road."

The first defendant to speak publicly provides details prosecutors do not have. King exposed himself, sexual horseplay commonly referred to in prison as "burning" someone, or trying to get them to "look at your thing." Parts of Brewer's story are amazingly believable. "I grabbed the can of spray paint and told him [King] that if he didn't stop, I was going to spray him." In Brewer's account, Byrd is quiet, except for another request. "Then Byrd came out [of the truck] and said, 'Let me smoke with you white boys,'" which might explain how Byrd and King ended up with DNA on the same cigarette butt.

Other admissions from Brewer do not match the Berry version. He claims it was an altercation between King and Byrd that started the attack, which he joined in: "I tried to kick Byrd and that's how I hurt my toe." Unsuccessful in thwarting the action, Brewer sprayed Byrd in the face and now offers another new detail, the strong reaction he claims King had: "'Don't do that! Don't spray nobody in the face!'"

Brewer pauses as if he's back in the woods. His voice breaks and quivers as his zigzag testimony forces comparisons to what the state has been able to piece together. Haltingly, yet still composed, Brewer faces the jury to demonstrate how Byrd had his hands up around his face because the spray paint was stinging, possibly blinding him. With hands around an ashen face, Brewer fires testimony that investigators do not have: "Shawn popped open his knife. Shawn cut his throat and Byrd fell."

Off the record, authorities have always conceded that Berry's knife-wielding reputation certainly meant he had no problem using his blade, but none will probably be convinced a story like this is true. Brewer finishes the wild tale, explaining with cool indifference how he got back in the truck to smoke a cigarette. "King got in to close the door. Then we heard the chain come out of the back of the truck, rattling, vibrating." His story also differs from previous statements Berry gave to the police on who drove— Brewer says that after Berry got behind the wheel, they took off, dragging the black man. He can't remember how far but testifies there was a quick stop to put the chain back on. He and Berry seem to agree the chain slipped off the victim; they just can't seem to agree about who jumped out to put it back on.

Brewer says he pleaded with Berry, "Man, you're not fixing to drag this man like you did that mailbox?" Brewer testifies that the ride continued and "everybody knew something had happened" when they passed the concrete culvert on Huff Creek Road. The something that had happened was the decapitation of James Byrd, Jr.

Out of reverence for his friend, John William King's name is barely mentioned for much of the final portion of Brewer's story. But he does finally assign King a minor role as the person who "took the chain off" at the graveyard. I have to wonder, when King hears what his fellow CKA member has testified to, will it make him what King once labeled Berry—*a snitch ass traitor?*

In what can only be considered an attempt to deny prosecutors an opportunity to show gruesome crime scene photos to Brewer, his own lawyers ask if he has seen the pictures of what happened to Byrd. Brewer is genuinely caught off guard. He throws his arms up in a defensive posture to cover his face, then turns his back with another batch of tears riding the corners of his eyes. "I don't want to look at those pictures." Layne Walker is cool, steps back, gives Brewer a chance to put his arms down and compose himself a second. "Did you mean for this to happen?" he asks. Again, Brewer makes it indisputably clear: "I do not want to look at those pictures."

Brewer sits alone in the witness box for several seconds before anyone from the prosecution table makes a move. At three-fifteen, Pat Hardy calmly begins, remaining seated. Yet the assistant DA is so angrily excited the small wooden chair can scarcely hold him. Hardy's voice has a hint of a little boy, a sliver of muffled joy at finally being let in the game. Now it's his turn to hit a home run.

For the next few minutes, the two reiterate items in Brewer's criminal record, personal life, and other things that lull the defendant into a false sense of security. Hardy's Southern-gentleman approach is being used to soften Brewer for the state's attack, which soon begins: "Permission to approach the witness, Your Honor."

In one split second, and about three long strides from the state's square table directly to Brewer's face, Hardy's whole demeanor changes. He is ready to tear Brewer to shreds with questions about Beto, the CKA, and the night of the murder. Impatient with the ball of confusion that Brewer appears to be, Hardy takes a run at the CKA: "Are you over your crying about the blood oath yet?" He follows up with a barrage of intense questions, then assumes a more intentional position in the courtroom, standing at an angle, as if to partially block Brewer's view of his attorneys. Finally, he gets Brewer to admit he was never sexually abused in prison. It is a grave contradiction to defense testimony and snatches away any empathy Brewer may have accrued.

Hardy zeroes in on Brewer's motivation for even being in Jasper.

Brewer blames it on a big fight between him and his girlfriend. Hardy obviously thinks there's more to it. "After you had your fight, did you tell Tammy you were going to Jasper to see someone who loved you?" Brewer looks stupefied and wants to get belligerent with Hardy. He responds gruffly, "I told her I was going to Bill King's house. I didn't say 'love.'"

Hardy, a forty-nine-year-old former bouncer turned narcotics officer, is a good 6 feet tall. At more than two hundred pounds, the imposing stance, honest stare, and cowboy background make him appear twice Brewer's size. Hardy is more than familiar with an interrogation technique known as "good cop, bad cop." He is successful in the convincing delivery of both. Brewer trembles on, nervous and forgetful, and changes parts of his story under fierce questioning.

Angrier than ever, Hardy shifts gears again and is on the logging road. He wants Brewer to go over certain portions of the dramatic episode already laid out for the jury. Brewer tenses up even more when Hardy does not buy the tidy business that the defendant's role in the dragging was almost nonexistent. A flurry of questions about the chain, his own fingerprints, whether Berry was right- or left-handed, and how he stabbed Byrd renders the Exalted Cyclops incapable of consistency with his previous defense testimony.

Brewer makes one mistake after another; one of the biggest is to provoke Hardy with eye contact when he assumes state questioning is near an end. "That's my story." With his raspy, East Texas intonation constantly rising, Hardy almost yells at Brewer, "That's your BIG Aryan story?" But it does not end there. When Hardy wants Brewer to confess that a kick to Byrd's head was how he actually got blood on his shoes, Brewer mumbles that it's a good question, one for which he has no believable explanation.

Hardy breathes in and out, steps back to the prosecution's table for a miniconference of maybe three seconds. He sits down. "Pass the witness, Your Honor."

The jury must consider five options: murder, capital murder, assault, aggravated assault, or they can vote to acquit.

Guy James Gray closes for the state with a stern reminder that all Brewer has done is lied and cried and that there are three things the jury must remember: the facts, the law, and the evidence. "There were three men in the truck, three pairs of shoes, three cigarette butts, and all three were involved." Three seats to the right of my assigned chair is Sonny Cribbs, perhaps here to compare notes.

Gray addresses the notion that Berry single-handedly committed the crime. "A chemist examined the shirt James Byrd was wearing. There was no blood on the shirt, just black spray paint." Gray strokes the absence of logic: "If Byrd's throat was cut the way Brewer described, wouldn't there have been a sea of blood on his clothing?"

Gray keeps his remarks short and talks about how much the defendant has in common with an inmate already on Texas' death row. "Russell Brewer is just exactly like Bill King, same tattoos, same lightning bolts, same neo-Nazi way of thinking. They discussed *The Turner Diaries* and different ways to kill blacks and stir up trouble."

Just before the DA from Jasper County sits down, he uses Brewer's own providential words from a letter, a boastful kite to King in jail—"A life sentence would do us no justice"—at which point the accused hangs his head lower.

Doug Barlow is next in line; he jumps up with great enthusiasm, eager to erase Gray's stinging words, as well as those from his client's own pen. Barlow vigilantly pleads with jurors to take certain pieces of seemingly incriminating evidence into deliberations so they can read parts of a letter that are scratched out. "We don't have the burden of proof, the state does."

Layne Walker then takes over for the defense. "I'm going to beg you to find that he was a racist, but that's not what he's here for." Walker looks the part of a young, successful lawyer: handsome, smart, and professionally dressed. Walker presents predeliberative instructions: "You have the right to request the transcript, send out a note, go through all the witnesses."

Walker sits down. A few seconds later, Guy James Gray rises again to give the finale, the state's response. Large bags under the DA's eyes make him look like a man on his last legs. He can barely be heard in the quiet courtroom. I sit on the edge of seat number 75 to witness his final burst of energy. Somehow, Gray musters the strength to project his fading voice. "It took all three to subdue James Byrd, one of them had to hold him down, so he's fighting with everything he has. There are three men out there and they are equally guilty."

Gray delivers one last charge to the jury before two alternates are officially released: "This case is your case. It belongs to the whole state of Texas. You are the law."

Judge Monte Lawlis returns to the chair to give directives. "I will not tolerate any disruptions once the verdict is read." He nods the okay to bring in the jury. It is two forty-eight when a bailiff instructs the jurors to enter. When they glide by, Brewer is visibly nervous, appears to tremble during the procession, then leans and whispers something to his lawyer. Finally, Brewer is ordered to stand and face his peers.

The judge looks at the paper, then reads the unanimous decision: "Guilty of capital murder." Brewer is stunned. Across the aisle,
Byrd family members are quiescent, reserved. It is not so much a
victory as it is vindication. There are no outbursts, and everyone
abides by Judge Lawlis' firm order. The jury walks out, but only
briefly. Three minutes pass; tired jurors are called right back. There
is one final decision to make in this trial—life or death. The state
presses ahead, victoriously and vehemently, into the penalty phase,
urging a death sentence as the only acceptable outcome.

Nine witnesses have their say on punishment for the state, with
the solid testimony of a psychiatrist the last that anxious jurors get
to hear. Anything Dr. Edward Gripon says, including his opinion
that Brewer is a future danger, is nearly eradicated because of the
very first witness defense attorneys call—Helen Brewer, mother of
the defendant.

The petite woman enters the courtroom crying, and every
mother's child in the vicinity knows this is not going to be easy, no
matter how they feel about Brewer or the horrific crime. In a display of common courtesy, John Stevens, Jr., the federal prosecutor,
stands to open the witness box. Tightly clutching her purse, she
sits, states her name for the record, wipes more tears, then appears
as ready as someone in her position can be. Unlike King, Brewer
does not ask if he can be removed for the difficult chore of watching his mother plead her case.

As Mrs. Brewer lovingly talks about her child, "Russell," the
defendant hangs his head to cry. This time, the tears are real. When
queried if she is here to ask the jury to spare his life, Mrs. Brewer
answers, "Yes sir, I am. He was in the wrong place at the wrong time
with the wrong crowd." She adds, "He went up there [to Jasper]
thinking that man [King] was his friend."

Prosecutors have no questions. They don't enjoy this at all. Neither does the Brewer family or any of the sympathetic spectators. Jurors also have long, sad faces. Guy James Gray appears to wrestle harder this time with his Catholic opposition to the death penalty, more so than he did in the first trial. His doses of premium whiskey and my dependence on antibiotics have dramatically increased. No one wants to hear a torn-up parent cry for the life of their child.

Inspired, the defense plans to plead, beg, cajole, do whatever they must to spare Brewer the death penalty. Attorneys present witness after witness, including a family friend, a cousin, Brewer's aunt, his father, and a surprising array of exhibits that have a profound impact on the jury.

Twelve color photos of the defendant—big blown-up poster boards—line every available space in the courtroom. The jumbo-size photo album depicts Brewer at various stages in his life. Observers sit up to look at the photos, particularly one of Brewer as a toddler. The display of humanity touches every person in the jury box, and one photo is more compelling than the rest—it is a preteen Brewer with his brother Mark. They have their arms around a little black kid.

Defense attorneys make Brewer more heart and soul, flesh and blood, than I thought possible. It is easy for people to hate King; he wants and craves that emotion for martyr status. But Brewer is like a little puppy who would simply be happy if someone paid him some attention.

As the recess for lunch begins, plenty of cameras and microphones record an unforgettable moment on the courthouse lawn. As they exit the building, two downcast families, in an unplanned encounter, exchange a few words. This time, it is the Brewer family that bravely approaches the victim's family. Highly emotional, some of the spoken words are unintelligible, but there are comments from the Brewers: "We'll get through this" and "We've got to look ahead." Then the father of Lawrence Russell Brewer says to the father of James Byrd, Jr., "Wish we could've met under different circumstances." There are tears. Tired members of each family embrace, then a small voice: "May God bless all of you and take care."

Though the somber moment seems deeply unsettling, some members of the Byrd family tell the mob of reporters they feel the pain Brewer's relatives are going through, and it helps.

Six hours after closing arguments in the penalty phase, the jury is still out. Panelists send out requests to see testimony and prison kites between King and Brewer. Time barely crawls. They are more thorough than anyone anticipates. Jurors also want definitions for the words "violence," "society," and "probability."

No one could predict that the case, at this juncture, would move at such a snail's pace, except longtime residents of Brazos County who have experience with the local criminal justice scene. Rumblings pour in from citizens who explain how the county is historically notorious for taking its time not only in capital cases, but in all kinds of cases. Jurors like to be fair. Journalists and prosecutors are politely warned not to think about going home anytime soon.

Back in the media room, many of the reporters are ready to pass out. Someone walks in and announces the jury wants dinner, after seven hours of deliberations—not a sign that a decision is near. Then Patty Reinert, a reporter for the *Houston Chronicle,* reminds everyone, "If someone was deciding my life, I guess I'd want them to take all the time in the world, take thirty days, whatever."

In the eleventh hour of deliberations, the jury sends out a note saying they are tired. Then an unconfirmed rumor follows—the panel is split 8 to 4. Officials do confirm that some of the jury members are having a lot of trouble with the first issue in the charge—future danger. For a capital conviction, they must unanimously answer yes to that question, and yes that they believe Brewer was aware Byrd would be killed, and no to the issue of mitigating factors like an abusive childhood or prison life.

District Attorney Guy James Gray looks wiped out. "It's very frustrating to get to this point and not be able to finish it out." But it is not the prosecution's call, nor the defense's. One decision is finally agreed upon—to come back fresh in the morning.

Deliberations resume on Thursday, September 23. The jury makes two requests; they want to see the controversial pictures of the tattoos, and also the family photo of Brewer, his mother, father, two brothers, and two sisters. According to some of the legal experts, this is not favorable to the state.

Ten minutes after the request for photos, two are allowed in. Back in the courtroom, Doug Barlow argues that all of the oversized photos should get a second look, but Judge Lawlis decides to grant only exhibit number 12 from the personal photos and exhibit number 102 of the tattoos.

At 11:07 A.M., Judge Lawlis shares the contents of a mysterious piece of white paper handed to him. "We cannot reach a decision according to instructions on issue number three." The defense wastes no time and immediately stands to ask Lawlis to sentence Brewer to life in prison. Obviously, Barlow and Walker, as do many members of the Brewer family and some in the media, read hope in the jury's action. The twelve oversized photos appear to have worked. Someone does not want to sentence Brewer to die.

Gray also stands to strongly object to any request that an automatic life sentence is the next step. "Your Honor, the tone and tenor of the note cannot be read as hopelessly deadlocked." Lawlis agrees and the motion is denied. The impartial judge sends the jury back his own response, which he reads aloud: "Please continue to deliberate until you cannot reach a verdict. Please continue your deliberations unless you tell me unequivocally, you are unable to answer issue number three, according to instructions."

After more than fourteen hours of intense, seesaw deliberations, a Brazos County jury that includes a businesswoman, a retiree, a contractor, and a Sunday-school teacher, unanimously agrees that Brewer must die for his role in the dragging of James Byrd, Jr. Lawlis reads their decision: "It is the order of the court that you, Lawrence Russell Brewer, the defendant herein, who has been judged to be guilty, is hereby sentenced to death by lethal injection." Lawlis then orders that Brewer promptly be delivered to the Texas Department of Criminal Justice.

As the decision is announced, Brewer purses his lips together and his mother wipes away a tear. There is no outburst of emotion from either family. Many are simply numb.

At a sea of microphones for one last media briefing on the courthouse lawn, the ninety-five degree humidity cooks exhausted prosecutors. Gray explains, "One person was the holdout and they [the other jurors] argued with him for a long time and he finally came around."

One reporter yells across the horde to ask Pat Hardy if he believes the death decision is "justice." Hardy's simple response is quoted around the world: "Nothing we could ever do to Lawrence Russell Brewer would ever give justice to James Byrd, Jr."

EIGHT

CBS Evening News anchor Dan Rather is in Jasper to meet a young man who claims he is different from the two roommates with whom he once lived and took a violently wrong turn.

Rather is easily recognized for his nightly news broadcast. The famous Texan is also right at home in this neck of the woods, not considered an outsider at all. His hometown of Wharton is just fifty miles southwest of Houston.

Rather enters the Jasper County Jail to tape an interview that will air on the CBS show *60 Minutes II*. As familiar East Texas hospitality is extended, Rather and company engage in small talk. Cameras are positioned; microphones are checked for sound. As Rather and Shawn Berry sit knee-to-knee in two metal folding chairs, a conversation with the third man accused in the dragging death of James Byrd, Jr., begins very simply, with Rather asking, "Shawn, tell me about yourself. Who are you?"

A month before jury selection for the third trial, I watch a riveting account of what Berry says happened to James Byrd, Jr. Berry claims he was frozen with fear, a sensation that allowed him to ride along in the center seat of his own truck as King took over the wheel for the dragging. Most surprising is a black man who appears on camera named Willie Land; he would trust Berry with anything he had. Rather's hard-hitting style is absent, and tough questions must've been edited out. Guy James Gray and Billy Rowles appear on camera for only about ninety seconds. The interview is a brilliant strategic move by the defense.

After Jasper County officials watch *60 Minutes II,* legal sparks begin to fly. They were under the impression that CBS would provide them with a copy of the unedited tapes. Then they saw the interview. Some blame Rowles for the fact that Jasper County did not have the jailhouse interview under surveillance to begin with, an accusation that creates one of the only visible cracks in an otherwise united prosecution front.

As usual, Guy James Gray steps up to shoulder responsibility, even though he was in Bryan trying to secure a capital conviction in the second trial. Not only does CBS refuse to hand over the entire interview, Mary Mapes, the Dallas-based producer of the segment, ignores a prosecution order to produce the tapes, which she claims are not in her possession.

Before I load my SUV with enough clothes to last for the two weeks I anticipate I'll be away for the third trial, I use my connections at CBS to try and contact Dan Rather. I want to know why this interview, why now, and how he came to be involved. His assistant, Kim Akhtar, tells me that Rather, on the advice of counsel, will not speak publicly about the interview, not even to another CBS employee. Listeners who missed the Tuesday night show call KRLD with questions. A few days later, my boss gets permission from New York to rebroadcast the interview on Dallas airwaves. Afterward, I join local talk show host Charley Jones in fielding calls and questions from opinionated listeners, many of whom don't believe Shawn Berry deserves a trial at all. Others express concern that Jasper has a hard enough row to hoe without a national interview that essentially allowed Berry to blame the crime on the other two, before a jury could be seated to hear all the details. A few don't see why it's so important for Jasper prosecutors to get into a fight with CBS; the evidence speaks for itself.

From the radio station, it is too far to drive home again. Since I am already packed, I immediately leave for Jasper. Nearly four hours later, I wonder about potential damage to the case as I take the last road into town, a lonely stretch of U.S. Highway 96 that's two lanes for too many miles to count.

Up ahead, I see an impatient idiot to the left and speak a word of warning aloud, "Don't you do it, big guy." Of course, he does. A logging truck fresh off some backwoods road suddenly pulls onto 96. He knows it is a dangerous thing to do, but he also knows that any smaller vehicle will automatically yield for the heavy load.

I slam on the brakes and veer to the right, just in case the car slides. I look at the truck again, curse the driver as he straightens directly in front of me, then gesture wildly—"Learn to drive!" I mumble a minute more, letting off steam.

I want to pass, but it is still a few miles to the next extended courtesy lane. Many blind spots and curves later, the trucker has built up his speed to about sixty-five miles per hour. He pushes the heavy cargo up to seventy and I back way off, dropping down to fifty-five. That's when something else catches my eye.

At the rear of the hauling truck are three or four bony logs that dangle off the back. A much closer inspection reveals the huge load is nowhere near secure. Hypnotized, I stay right behind the truck. While the logs, dozens of them, bounce and roll, I back off a little more. There are no other cars or trucks on our side of the highway. As we drive on, my nose starts to twitch. Suddenly, I notice the faint smell of something burning. Probably trash in the woods, I think, but I don't see any smoke. Heavy logs continue to shake and rattle, and threaten to cascade off the truck, spill all over the road, and crash into my Jeep.

The sensation that something is burning becomes gradually stronger and, seconds later, through a slightly opened window, the smell is undeniable. I see that three or four extra-long logs suspended over the truck are being dragged behind it. The logs produce tiny sparks as the driver flies down the highway.

At that exact moment, I see James Byrd, Jr., and feel the flame of his pain, a body not made of wood, but flesh, blood, and bone. I start to cry but manage to keep my eyes on the fiery flash that resembles a giant match being struck on the pavement. The logs pop and cackle. Dumbfounded, I watch and imagine those same logs are the body parts of a man whose life was taken because white men so full of hatred wanted to send a message and "die proudly" as stars in their movement, "heroes of the day."

The trucker finally turns off. I drive on, into Jasper, ready to hear why a third man stayed to watch.

Legal analysts underestimate the publicity left in the wake of the *60 Minutes II* interview. I cannot believe the delays and maneuvering that stem from the controversial interview. One reason for the delays is that the state is determined to examine what got edited out of the finished product—a lopsided interview that casts Berry in a largely sympathetic light, just four weeks before jury selection.

Attention that might have been reserved for the jury pool of five hundred Jasper County residents is instead focused on pretrial hearings and subpoenas aimed at anyone who might be in possession of three hours of tape, which, when edited, turned into the eighteen-minute interview that has jeopardized this trial.

An attorney who is no stranger to high-profile Texas cases represents Mary Mapes. Charles L. "Chip" Babcock, who defended Oprah in her fight against Texas beef producers, argues violation of First Amendment rights, which are now invoked to protect her work. Her defenders say a subpoena was served on the wrong party; instead of Mapes, they claim CBS is the sole proprietor of the tapes. Judge Joe Bob Golden is not happy to hear the reason Mapes did not attend a hearing with counsel—she took "a wrong turn" on her way to Jasper.

Mapes is hit with another deadline to turn over the written transcript, of which she admits to having a copy. When she refuses, a stay from an appeals court narrowly prevents Mapes from joining Berry in the Jasper County Jail. Prosecutors waste no time making a request to a New York judge when Mapes gives the name of the person she says was last seen with the tapes—Dan Rather. CBS vows to fight all attempts to get the unedited tapes or to put Rather on the witness stand. The East Coast judge must decide whether he will grant the Jasper DA's request to subpoena Rather.

For days, the saga goes from Golden's courtroom, to the jail, where Mapes posts a $2,000 bond to avoid incarceration, then to a Texas appeals court, New York, and back again. Meanwhile, not many pay attention to jury selection. Just moments before an all-white jury is officially selected and sworn in, Berry's attorney, Joseph C. "Lum" Hawthorn, files a surprise motion to move the trial. Opening statements are put on hold; Hawthorn claims his client cannot get a fair trial because of extensive publicity over the fight with CBS. Most of the fidgety reporters are upset with Hawthorn, especially since he is suspected of arranging the same national interview responsible for this so-called "pre-trial publicity" conundrum.

Judge Golden spends another off day sorting through a massive amount of broadcast and print stories to determine if Hawthorn's request merits a change of venue. While idle reporters ponder the possibility of packing up enough equipment to furnish a small city, there is sentiment among the ranks that Hawthorn's cries of unfair coverage will be ignored, that there is a better chance people in hell will get ice water.

Without comment, an appellate court refuses to overturn two contempt charges against Mapes. Her bond is revoked and she is again ordered to turn over the tapes and transcript or go to jail. "If she doesn't," Guy James Gray says, "she'll stay in jail until this trial is over or until she turns the material over."

On Wednesday morning, November 10, 1999, Jasper County officials ready a cell for Mary Mapes. As the clock ticks for the CBS producer, Judge Joe Bob Golden steps up, without the traditional black robe, and takes the bench around eight-thirty. Golden looks out on the pensive faces and frayed nerves of people from all sides who have been kept waiting.

Without expression, Golden denies the defense motion for a change of venue. He gives a one-sentence opinion on the matter, telling both sides it was filed for purposes of delay. The trial will go on. Journalists sigh. The Byrd family appear grateful, and artists prepare to sketch quizzical faces and animated gestures for those on both sides of the case.

Just after nine, the jury is ushered in and the state reads its capital murder indictment. Shawn Allen Berry stands to listen and face the judge. At the appropriate interval, he pleads, "Not guilty."

As the now twenty-four-year-old takes his seat, Judge Golden sternly gives instructions to the jury: "Do not read the paper, watch television, or listen to the radio, or talk with family members about this trial. I will not permit taking notes by the jury."

Guy James Gray's haggard demeanor betrays him. He wears the case on his face. Seventeen long, hard months have aged Gray, which is apparent when he opens his mouth to speak. "This boy, sitting over here"—he spins and points at Berry—"is not the same as the other two." This hometown jury is also not the same as the other two. The gender makeup on this panel is reversed. This time, there are seven women and five men. The female jurors may have something else in common besides being neighbors—not one of them is too young to be a mother, perhaps a mother to a son not unlike Berry in age and physical characteristics.

Living up to his name, Gray develops a strand or two of noticeable silver in various places on his head. With a larger black mane to work with, I am able to hide new gray hairs that threaten to emerge from an impromptu part on the side. Since the first trial, my thinning hair falls out so fast that my stylist is concerned I may soon need a weave or a wig. Loss of hair, headaches, nausea, and nightmares—these are constant signs that my body can't fully absorb all the stress of this case, signs that I am not impervious to the sting of racism. In Bryan, few people knew it, but I was sick every day of the trial. Besides hair and stress, Gray and I have something else in common. Gray confides to a few of us that he does not sleep well. For the DA, and for me, there is a glimmer of hope that rest will follow closure.

Gray tells the hometown jury that Berry's codefendants John William King and Lawrence Russell Brewer constantly talked about a return to the "old days of dragging and lynching blacks." Gray whirls around as his words burn with invisible adrenaline: "The choice to pick up James Byrd, Jr., on MLK was made by Shawn Berry."

At one point, Gray innocently asks a seemingly loaded question, "Who precipitated this?" Again, Gray points out a defense strategy from the *60 Minutes II* interview—Berry isn't a racist and doesn't have racist tattoos, but, according to Gray, "He was living with them [racists]." Gray even offers an idea about the attraction of such an association: "He may have been a thrill seeker who wanted to pick up a rattlesnake to see what would happen."

For a man who rarely speaks above a whisper and prefers not to use fire to convey his message, the comment is not lost on anyone in the courtroom. More than once, he calls Berry an "active participant" who made a choice to pick up a black man despite full knowledge of his friends' attitudes toward African-Americans. Gray also promises to show, from clothes and shoe print evidence, that all three men played a role in the murder. Gray then concentrates on seven incriminating firsthand accounts Berry gave to authorities after his arrest. "Credibility is an issue in this trial."

Berry is straight as an arrow. Dressed in a nice navy sport coat, he is the center of attention at the front of the courtroom. His dark hair is cut short, almost a buzz cut. Gone is the scruffy goatee. If anything, Berry looks like a regretful soldier in a military tribunal who waits to hear if he will get a slap on the wrist or maybe sixty days in the stockade.

Berry is even paler than King or Brewer, with a sweet face the color of buttermilk. Berry looks slimmer than his listed prison weight of 160 pounds, in contrast to the noticeable weight gains of King and Brewer. He is keenly aware that his every move is being scrutinized and documented by the world press. Berry has probably spent a large chunk of his life in a somewhat aggressive, overcompensatory mode to make up for his lack of height.

Near the end of Gray's opening statement, Berry leans over to whisper something important to his lawyer. Lum Hawthorn hears it but remains focused on Gray. This is the only trial where the defense is not joined by cocounsel. It is Hawthorn's ballgame—he calls the shots and even gets approval to have a lay person sit at the defense table.

Smugly seated on the other side of Berry is his fiancée, Christie Marcontell. She looks oddly out of place and is the recipient of more than a few cold stares from the opposite side of the room. The mother of Berry's only child, she takes notes, smiles, touches Berry every so often. The jury likes her. Hell, some of them probably know her.

Hawthorn makes brief, rapid-fire remarks. He is a man unafraid to take calculated chances, as is clear from his decision to agree to the Dan Rather interview, his hasty change-of-venue motion, and his decision to bring Berry's fiancée to the defense table.

Hawthorn talks much louder than Gray as he sets out to respond to many of the state's charges with one of his own. What the prosecution has done, according to Hawthorn, is "weave a tale of guilt by association."

Louis Berry sits directly behind his younger brother, on the first spectator row, like they are entwined from back to chest. As Hawthorn speaks, it is as if the free Berry is on trial, more so than his brother. After all, he was able to get away from King, but didn't save his sibling in time.

Hawthorn pummels the raw issue of association: "King wasn't a racist until after he was in prison and he met Brewer," then he adds, "Berry didn't believe King was an avowed racist." Hawthorn tells the jury that Brewer's arrival in town about three weeks before the murder is the catalyst that stirs up "old prison trash talk." He gives the jury a free sample: "They used the *n* word, but Shawn thought it was just talk."

One of the provocative things Hawthorn promises, including answers about why Berry picked up the victim, why blood is on his clothing, and why he didn't go to the police, is that the defense attorney will deliver Berry to the stand so they can hear the full story of what happened the night James Byrd, Jr., was dragged to death. It is an exciting pledge, a way for Hawthorn to make a covenant with this jury—"I promise you can look at him square in the eye." But as I look square in the eyes of serious white faces that make up this panel, I can't help but wonder who among them has not already heard Berry's televised testimony four weeks ago when he conveniently blamed the murder on King and Brewer.

As proceedings kick into high gear, a deal is reached to keep Mary Mapes, the CBS sacrificial lamb, out of the Jasper County Jail. As part of the agreement, all subpoenas for Dan Rather will be withdrawn. During the morning break, a polished network attorney stands underneath large, shady pecan trees on the courthouse lawn and confirms that a full transcript of the interview with Shawn Berry will be posted on the Internet for all the world to see.

"Both sides are tired of the side show," he continues. "It is time to move on."

Keisha Adkins, the first witness for the state, is tired of doing this. Not much in her blasé tone and lukewarm mannerisms have changed. Her stringy brown hair looks the same. She appears to know the drill. Once again, she nails the defendant: "Shawn was driving." Adkins is followed by another familiar face. Billy Mahathay is briefly questioned by the district attorney about a house party attended by several people on Saturday night, June 6, 1998. Again, Mahathay confirms the last time he saw his boyhood friend alive. "Mr. Byrd left walking, walking on the side of the road."

Because I've heard, repeated, and reported it so often, I've nearly memorized the testimony. Witness number three, Steven Scott, tells the Berry jury the same thing he told the other two: "He was staggering all over the road." A honey-faced kid, now nineteen years old, Scott maintains he simply followed his heart when he didn't pick Byrd up. I stop writing. Anyone who has covered the previous trials knows that Scott was in a big hurry to get to his mother's house that Saturday night. When he does, he's just arrived at the front porch, where he sees the driver of a step-side truck cruise right by. Scott looks at his third jury: "I saw Mr. Byrd pass by riding on the back of a truck."

After Adkins, Mahathay, and Scott, the witness order changes. Here the prosecution begins to set in motion a counterstrategy that will help highlight stark differences between the actions of this defendant and the other two. It is not necessary to bring out the heavy artillery yet, like crime scene photos, because Berry must be handled with a certain amount of finesse. First, the state introduces its new witness lineup with Larry Douglas Pulliam, the officer who arrested Berry. Next up is Curtis Frame, the man considered the primary caretaker of all the state's evidence, and one of the lead investigators on this case.

When asked about Berry's attitude and behavior, Frame looks at the jury. "I think he was more afraid for himself than of the two defendants." Studious and smart, he dons round, Gandhi-like glasses and is mostly bald. He is nervous, knowing Hawthorn can't wait to poke holes in any part of his testimony.

The defense attorney has done his homework. The cross-examination produces the first mien of shock when Hawthorn demands to see the chain. A lull falls over the courtroom. No one can imagine what motivates Berry's lawyer to bring the chain out on the first day of testimony. This is also the only time a defense attorney has asked to hold the chain.

After Hawthorn presents the 24½-foot-long chain as evidence, he asks Frame to officially identify it. Then Hawthorn asks Frame to assist him in stretching out the chain. It is clear Hawthorn has studied notes on the first two trials. Frame looks around at prosecutors. There is no real objection unless there are legal grounds for stopping Hawthorn from unequivocally stealing the state's thunder.

The loud, clanking chain makes everyone uneasy. As two men on opposite teams extend it, the jury watches. With Hawthorn's hands all over the chain, it is not as big and frightening to this jury as it was to the previous two. Hawthorn, in one strategic objective, takes away the state's most dramatic piece of evidence by not only introducing it with one of their witnesses, but by also demonstratively holding it so that its implied terror is attenuated. Hawthorn wants jurors to see there is nothing to be afraid of. He makes the point that Berry should not be convicted for mere ownership of a log chain.

More investigators take the stand as the state's cavalcade of witnesses spew out damaging testimony about Berry, a man who rejected a plea agreement for life so he, according to Marcontell, could prove his innocence in court.

From Billy Rowles to excerpts from the *60 Minutes II* interview, the state focus turns to a fuzzy shoe print, one they claim was made on the passenger side of the truck by a tennis shoe, not by the polo boots Berry was wearing. If King was driving during the dragging, as Berry told Dan Rather, then why was his shoe print—and not Berry's—outside the truck on the passenger side when it came to a halt?

Prosecutors are adamant that Berry drove his own truck, which is why investigators could not find a match on the road for the shoes he wore. Again and again, they plant the seed that once Byrd was chained to the truck, the driver did not get out after the dragging began. King wore sandals; Brewer had on tennis shoes. A sandal print was discovered early in the case; the partial tennis-shoe print was discovered later. Nonetheless, it gives prosecutors ammunition that place King and Brewer outside the truck, on the passenger side. They say there is a reason Berry's shoe print was never found—he was behind the wheel.

When the grisly crime scene photos are produced, Betty Boatner and Stella Brumley quietly leave the courtroom to avoid what they know is next: the shattering synopsis from the state's best witness, Dr. Tommy Brown, the forensic pathologist. Five minutes after he takes the witness chair, Brown describes for the jury the surface of Huff Creek Road, and the concrete culvert. He directs them at the appropriate times to "turn the page." Some do, a couple do not. One juror just gives up, he closes the photo book and Dr. Brown continues.

For much of the difficult testimony, Berry keeps his head lowered looking at the defense table where his forearms rest and fingers on both hands crisscross in prayer. Christie Marcontell places her hand to her mouth when Dr. Brown asserts his belief that Byrd "was alive and trying to alleviate the excruciating pain."

The state does not show the chain, since Hawthorn has beaten them to it. The expected drama from the state's triple threat of the chain, Dr. Brown, and the video is reduced. But the doctor makes believers of all. He does not need the chain. His descriptive testimony is still effective and allows this jury, like the other two, to hear the chain fall to the ground, clink down an old logging road, and tighten around the ankles of a human being. They listen closely and perhaps even hear it being loosened and thrown back into Berry's old truck.

After a fifteen-minute recess, the state announces itself ready to show the jury a tape of Huff Creek Road. Hawthorn looks bewildered, especially since he has already strategically "borrowed" a video from the state's collection to share with the jury. More thunder he attempted to steal. Hawthorn probably does not know, until this minute, that it was the wrong video.

Prosecutors certainly did sit still when he unraveled the log chain first, but there was no way they were going to volunteer which tape Hawthorn should've been in the hunt for. So they gave him one that was less clear, more grainy and uneven, and not the scariest part of the route. Now the state puts Clifton Orr on the stand in case there are questions about evidence recovered from the road. They play the *correct* silent movie.

Just as the lights are dimmed, everyone sits at attention to mentally deposit their bodies in the gray truck. It is almost three o'clock on a beautiful Friday afternoon in Jasper; the silence rolls on, vividly clear, accompanied by deafening bells from the clock tower that tops the courthouse. Three bells sound special music for a dragging, one for each accused man.

Seventeen minutes after both sides huddle next to Judge Joe Bob Golden's bench, the defense calls its first witness. The name is a surprise for anyone who has monitored this case.

Dr. Edward Gripon, the same forensic psychiatrist who testified for the state in the penalty phase of the King and Brewer trials, looks like he woke up on the wrong side of the bed for this one. Gripon is nowhere near the fireball of confidence he was in the other trials.

To get it on the record, Gripon tells the jury about his past affiliation with the case. Gripon quickly confirms that the state did contact him to work on the Berry trial but that he, in good conscience, could not do so. He appears to wrestle with something that he can't, or doesn't quite know how, to express. The lone fact that he chooses to testify for the defense sends an earsplitting message to the jury: Berry is so completely different from his racist cohorts that even a psychiatrist who is paid for his expert opinion cannot bring himself to testify against him. "I did not find Shawn Allen Berry to be a racist."

The state gets burned, unprepared for Gripon, who largely reiterates and strengthens what Hawthorn says in his opening statement—Berry is not a thrill seeker, a racist, or a person with derogatory attitudes toward blacks.

On cross-examination, when Guy James Gray asks what prompted Berry to pick up a black man at 2 A.M., Gripon casually chalks it up to "relatively poor judgment." Gray presses Gripon a little harder. "Considering his [codefendants'] feelings about black people?" to which, falling right into the state's trap, the doctor replies, "If he took seriously what they said, then one would draw the conclusion Shawn Allen Berry's intent was to hurt James Byrd, Jr."

Other things backfire. Gripon carelessly admits that "in the presence of alcohol, Shawn might lose his temper." The DA then inquires if Gripon even bothered to ask Berry if he had a knife that night. Gripon did not. Gray is curious what the outcome would've been if he had. "He could've chosen to use it," Gripon answers.

Witness number two, Dr. Lynn Pearson, an orthopedic surgeon, is another ace up Hawthorn's sleeve. On June 4, 1998, just three days before the murder, Berry saw Pearson to have his fractured hand removed from a splint that was put on three weeks earlier. Hawthorn suggests that Berry might have had trouble lifting a chain with his dominant right hand. Gray, in his cross-examination, counters that alcohol could dull the pain, a premise that Pearson concedes as possible. Gray plants the seed that a May domestic altercation with Marcontell is how Berry injured his right hand, which, he says, had enough time to heal so that Berry could have been an "active participant" in the June dragging.

Most of the reporters do not see Hawthorn's advance witness list. At one of the news briefings, the defense attorney only mentions his client and a blood-spatter expert as probable witnesses. Jurors are treated to many more. Next, they hear from an elderly gentleman, the grandfather of Christie Marcontell. She and Berry lived with the old man for a time. He adds very little to the mix. But Hawthorn uses Elmer Marcontell to establish a particular pattern. "Notice any racist tendencies?" "Did he have black friends?" "Ever make derogatory remarks about black people?" Most locals following the case already know Berry did indeed have black friends and coworkers. Those who did not know discovered as much in the CBS interview.

Witness number four is on fire to help—he is the defendant's only brother, Louis Michael Berry. In the first and second trials, he made a premium witness for the state. Just before this trial started, Assistant DA Pat Hardy explained why he would not be called a third time: "No one expects Louis to testify against his brother."

The now twenty-six-year-old is better-looking than the defendant, though there is a strong resemblance. Despite how much he, like his younger brother, smokes and drinks, drives fast and lives hard, there is something sensitive about Louis Berry, something that makes him poetically tragic. He comes across as the kind of guy who would forgo wealth and a life of luxury if he could not bring his little brother along for the trip.

Berry speaks consistently and deliberately, mostly about his brother's perceived temper and the alleged knife fights that are being mentioned by prosecutors. Berry does not want to say anything to injure defense chances for a lesser charge, if not outright acquittal. The conversation quickly turns to Bill King and his fanatical views, which Berry testifies were a lot of hot air. Of the movie *Schindler's List,* Berry repeats King's so-called theory: "It's a bitch-ass Jewish view, it didn't happen." Then, Berry tells the jury, "He tried to sell us on it but we weren't buying into it, so he toned it way down." Pain fills the deep booming voice; he is not quite sure he can save his brother from the once charismatic clutches of John William King.

After Berry's testimony, Brit Featherston, a Lufkin, Texas–based assistant U.S. attorney who joined the case in Bryan, realizes that the jury likes Berry. They learn that he is one of the few friends in the clique that finally stands up to King, particularly after he disrespects a black friend. There are no prosecution points to score here.

A friend of the defendant's is the next witness. He understands the drill, the three answers in particular that will aid Berry the most. It is established, witness after witness, that Berry helped black people by giving them rides, even taking shortcuts through back roads to avoid incidents in town, that he was not a racist, and that he did have black associates. Even an African-American man who worked with Berry at Jasper Tire takes the stand to say his white friend had never made derogatory remarks about black people around him, and that Berry cried at the funeral of a black friend. Joe Glenn has no other choice under Gray's cross-examination than to answer in the affirmative when Gray asks, "Are you surprised that he lived with two racists?"

Before Gray can pose his last question, the courthouse clock strikes noon. After the twelfth bell, Judge Golden orders a recess.

Much of Christie Marcontell's time on the stand amounts to an openly flirtatious exchange with the jury. She is pretty and wears nice clothes. But heavy makeup for a twenty-two-year-old detracts from Marcontell's natural glow. She reiterates what most of the witnesses have already said: "Shawn is not a racist."

Marcontell's childish comments about the stormy side of their relationship do not help his image much, but she gets credit for trying. "Me and Shawn enjoyed fighting. Both of us were jealous. I love him with all my heart and I know he loves me." She needs a buffer to explain a sorry criminal-mischief complaint she filed against him. "Shawn and I were dating, one night he didn't come home. I found him at a motel, broke into his truck, and tore some stuff up." The whole time his fiancée talks, Berry nervously fidgets. It is dirty laundry he'd rather not air in public, especially since the state has already beaten them to it. Marcontell admits that portions of her story about a vicious attack, in which Berry allegedly abused her, were made up. "This is stupid on my part. You shouldn't play with the law."

Despite her intentions to show the gentle, caring side of her man, Marcontell comes across as a young woman who allowed Berry to push and shove, slap and cheat on her. It makes it look as if there may be some truth to the state's contention that Berry always carries a knife and never backs away from a fight, not even one with someone he loves.

By midafternoon, the courtroom is packed. All these spectators know Berry's turn is near. Hawthorn has gone well over the "two" promised witnesses. But he isn't done with courtroom theatrics. Witness number sixteen is an attractive black woman who enters from the small corridor when she hears her name.

Ann-Marie Norman's British accent is unmistakable, prompting several questions about what kind of route leads from England to Jasper. The petite twenty-something woman confirms her homeland but has lived in Jasper seven years. Her high-yellow, or "fair," skin tone is the first clue that she is the product of an interracial relationship—her mother is white and her father black. Norman, a close friend of Berry's, works as a bank teller. But it is not her unwavering devotion to Berry as a friend that garners the most attention from residents and reporters. It is what she has to say about John William King.

"I met Bill King at Wal-Mart. I've been to his apartment," Norman emphatically states. With her full features, dark wavy hair, and beautiful color, Norman is engaging. She says that she nonchalantly told King to let her cop "a fag or two." After she explains that "fags" is British slang for "smokes," laughter fills the courtroom. Norman says King was nice and showed no reaction to her race while she was at his apartment. This prompts more laughter. No one can ever recall a single witness who described King as nice. Jurors are treated to "evil," "satanic," and "mean to the core," but never "nice."

It appears Hawthorn uses Norman to prove his client had no fear in placing a black person directly in King's path. Norman says she let King know her feelings about his prison art. "I told him his tattoos were offensive to me, and he told me he had to get them in prison."

For his nineteenth and twentieth witnesses, Hawthorn finally provides the jury the promised expert testimony. First up, Dr. Lloyd White, a medical examiner from Corpus Christi, Texas, says Tommy Brown cannot prove Byrd was "alive and conscious" for part of the dragging. White simply disagrees that Brown's conclusions based on certain injuries are enough to deduce Byrd was conscious.

Paulette Sutton is an impressive forensic serologist from Memphis. Sutton infiltrated the reporters' hangout for lunch, never once revealing herself as Hawthorn's much anticipated blood expert. She played the role of little lost traveler. Maybe she really was. Sutton has impeccable credentials, including training with the FBI Academy. Her main job was to test the stains on Berry's boots and clothing. Sutton is not on the stand long before she confidently proclaims, "The type of stain on the items are not consistent with what we consider a beating or assault." Dozens who listen to and observe her scientific conclusions are impressed: The stain on Berry's jeans is a diluted stain, one she suggests is consistent with "washing a chain, not participating in a murder."

Guy James Gray rises to do the state's difficult cross-examination. Slowly, he searches his mind for ways to poke holes in her educated theories. "What kind of jeans did you work with?" She knows where Gray heads and agrees color can make a difference in test results.

The overflow crowd takes forever to drain out of the half-glass double doors, the courtroom's lone public exit. At the defense rail that separates family from the defendant, anyone in earshot can hear the discussion. Berry and his supporters critique the testimony and Hawthorn's performance. They believe it went well.

At 10 A.M. on Tuesday, November 16, Shawn Allen Berry is sworn in, raising the same right hand that a doctor swears might've been wracked with pain the night of the attack.

The exchange begins with Hawthorn trying to settle his young client down. He drops his usual rapid-fire delivery. "Were you nervous when you gave your statements?" Berry responds, "Yes, I was." Berry admits he was also nervous when he spoke with Dan Rather for the *60 Minutes II* interview. He is nervous right now. His life hangs in the balance, hinges on every word, expression, or pause.

"Tell the jury what happened," Hawthorn instructs his apprehensive client. "I want you to look at the jury, Shawn." Like a contrite misbehaver, Berry turns to face the jury and begins to talk about his background. They see a younger Berry, someone who grew up among them, a cute kid who made some mistakes.

"My mom wasn't very responsible. She was always out and I was told she was wild." Berry uses the same kind of language to describe her that prosecutors use when describing him as a thrill seeker.

Many female jurors are saddened that Berry is, for all intents and purposes, still a boy without a mother. When Berry speaks about an event many locals have never forgotten, the suicide of his stepfather, there is even more sympathy for him. After all, this is a hometown boy some residents personally know for his untamable wild streak, but also for his talent for patiently carving handmade rocking horses and intricate figurines. Berry is the man-child who greeted countless citizens at the only movie theater in town, but at the same time a person fathers might lock their daughters away from on a Saturday night.

If it takes a village to raise a child, these jurors surely represent the very people who brought this boy up; they cannot help but be affected by what went wrong in an idyllic town that prides itself on being in touch with faith and values. There are more than fifty churches here, more than enough help for those who are in need, or hurting. Berry's voice cracks in a touching soliloquy he gives about the father who commits suicide. "He died on Huff Creek Road."

The reserved front-row seat where Louis Berry normally sits appears empty. It is not. Berry is hunched over so far down, with elbows propped on his knees, that he is just barely on the edge of the bench. The entire display of unspoken affection between the two has a tremendous impact on the jury. Louis offers Shawn Berry all that he has: smiles, eye contact, and support.

Berry explains how Donald Hopson's suicide became the pivotal point that made his tough-luck life even worse. He testifies about the downhill ride of poor grades, a string of jobs, how he met Bill King, and the unlocked warehouse the pair burglarized. It lasts for several minutes.

Enthralled jurors are on an emotional seesaw with Berry. When he talks about King, all sympathy for him evaporates. When he outlines second chances he takes to turn his life around, Berry is almost admirable. Perhaps they see the talented younger Berry many knew for his championship rodeo potential and strong work ethic. It is his friendship with King that vexes them. If the defense theories are right, Berry does not realize, until it is too late, that King is incorrigible.

Berry virtually ignored what seems like clue after clue following King's release from prison. When Berry tried to help his friend find gainful employment, King showed up in a tank top shirt. Berry's employer saw the tattoos and refused to hire him. Berry admits race was all King talked about. "Every other word out of his mouth was the *n* word and how he couldn't stand Jewish people. And he talked about *The Turner Diaries*." Then, Berry looks embarrassingly at the jury: "King said there was going to be an uprising and they'd hang so many of them [blacks] they'd run out of rope."

Now Berry testifies about other disturbing clues that should've served as red flags. "Everything he said was very negative, and we never paid any attention to it." Hindsight being twenty-twenty, Berry realizes what a grave mistake that was.

Hawthorn flips back to the subject of tattoos. "Why would you run around with someone with tattoos like that?" Berry's answer convinces no one. "I didn't really think much of it. I thought it was the same old Bill." Three weeks before the murder, when Russell Brewer came to town for a visit, Berry didn't get a good vibe. "Bill instantly changed when Brewer got to town." Still, he did not move out.

An hour and fifteen minutes after Berry takes the stand, the story builds to the events of June 1998. Berry confirms what Keisha Adkins has said. All three men did get in his truck to leave at the same time. "I was driving." Like Brewer's version, Berry has many of the same highlights, including the stop at BJ's store, where he acknowledges there was a switch in where everyone, except him, would ride.

From his perspective in the cab with the victim, Berry is able to offer details not heard in the Rather interview or from Brewer. "I gave him another beer while he was in the cab; I gave him a cigarette"—which is another possible explanation for Byrd's DNA on one of the butts found at the crime scene. Berry says he turned onto FM 1408, and King instructed him to "take the Baha trail," King-slang for the logging road.

Following orders, Berry says the four of them were off-roading for a while. Berry also makes it clear that it was King's idea to go down there and that he was in no position to hear what King and Brewer were plotting on the back of the truck. Once they ventured into the deeper woods on the logging road, Berry says his passenger turned to him and asked, "Where we going?" Not long after, the truck was partially swallowed by a giant dirt pocket. Berry says they were briefly stuck, so King and Brewer got out to push the truck from the sandy pit. Then, Berry takes his hand to demonstrate on the witness stand. "King hit on top of the truck and told me to stop for a minute." Berry bangs his fist three times.

King jumped over the side of the truck, Brewer off the back. Berry also has his story down pat and continues to talk about how

King and Brewer pulled Byrd, who was yelling for them to stop, to the ground. Berry blames them; Brewer blames him. Berry tells the spellbound jury that the entire attack caught him off guard and he ran around to try and stop King. That's when he heard the angry King charge, "Fuck it. Let's kill this nigger." Berry says he got in between the two men and pleaded with them to stop. "Bill said the same thing could happen to a nigger lover."

For someone who claims to have only listened in paralyzed fear, unable to see what happened, Berry certainly saw something. "I don't remember how they got him to the ground. Bill and Russell may have been hitting him with fists. When he was on the ground, they were kicking him with their feet." Berry loudly snaps his finger for emphasis. "To me it was quick." When she hears Berry's flip answer to how long the struggle lasted, Betty Boatner gets up and leaves the courtroom.

On advice from his counsel, Berry again makes a conscious effort to look at the jury so they can see his eyes. The mostly female panel stare back with the same intensity. "It didn't end there. Somehow he got to his feet. He may have tried to run. I remember seeing Mr. Byrd run in my direction. They pushed him, I jumped back, and something brushed my right leg."

Berry has a number of details, all of which serve to support his claim of being an innocent bystander and how blood may have ended up on his clothes and shoes. "They took him to the back of the truck to beat him."

Berry finishes up when he testifies about how the victim wound up on his hands and knees. "They were hitting him, kicking him. Russell found a can of spray paint in the back of the truck." Berry confirms Brewer did spray Byrd in the face with the black paint, and that Brewer kicked Byrd so hard in the head that "he didn't move at all, he never moved again." Shamefaced, he confesses, "That's when I realized my pants were wet."

Berry pauses several times to survey the faces of jury members and to gauge the impact of his own exasperated sorrow. "A chain got drug out of the back of my truck." Berry says King then slid onto the driver's side, and Brewer got in on the passenger side, leaving him sandwiched in the middle. He looks at the jury. "They started dragging him." *They*. Berry's voice slows. He sounds more remorseful, is thoughtful in the selection of words. Berry blames everybody but himself. There are no tears as he calmly tells jurors it was King who backed over the victim. "I believe Mr. Byrd was under the truck." His dramatic testimony stops for the loud chimes from the courthouse tower.

After the last strike, Berry resumes: "They got out, chained him back up. King is still driving. He took a left turn on Huff Creek Road." Hawthorn asks why Berry does not just tell them to stop. Berry turns to face the jury again. "I did ask them to stop and Bill King called me a ho." As King and Brewer, according to Berry, excitedly continued the drive, "laughing and giggling," he didn't say a word.

Berry's big brown eyes work in his favor when he offers the belief that he was, by being there, just as guilty as they were. The jury will have the final say on that.

When Hawthorn asks if he intentionally caused the death of James Byrd, Jr., Berry answers strongly, clearly, "No, I did not."

"In written statements, forty-five times you used the word 'we.' On *60 Minutes II,* you used the word 'they.' Was that a conscious shift?"

Berry has monitored two trials and looks more polished than

the state gives him credit for. "I used 'they,' but investigators wrote 'we' in the statements." He is ready for Guy James Gray. Berry even gets a little cocky under cross-examination, feels he is doing well on the stand. He can relax some, let his strict guard down.

Gray moves to the issue of who drank what and makes sure the jury knows that all the beer consumed that Saturday night was stolen from Solley's. Berry admits, "I drank four or five," and that he had a good idea it was stolen, along with some meat from Patrick's. Berry takes no responsibility for the stolen goods or how they got to King's apartment. Gray politely pounces on Berry. "Is this a pattern? Present but didn't know intent?" Berry responds weakly, "No, I don't believe so."

As things wind down, Hawthorn pulls off one more strategic coup. He directs the jury's attention to the overhead projector's bright white screen. It is a mug shot of his client, scraggly and tanned, almost unrecognizable in prison getup, longer hair, and an unkempt goatee. Then, suddenly, without warning, the state is again caught off guard as Hawthorn slips in a color picture of the defendant with his little toddler son, Montana.

Hawthorn asks Berry to identify the larger-than-life photo. He lovingly looks at the cute baby boy. He smiles at the jury with pride and tells them it is his son. The message is a powerful image for the seven-woman, five-man jury. They now see the young child who would be deprived of a father if Berry is sentenced to life *or* death.

At almost 4 P.M., the defense rests. After a total of five hours, Shawn Allen Berry leaves the stand a confident young man, one who finally expresses relief as he nears his brother. Christie Marcontell beams with pride, touching Berry when he sits back down— nothing too demonstrative; they do not dare celebrate in front of the jury. But Berry has done well on the stand and they know it.

Rebuttal testimony begins immediately. One of the witnesses is the same twenty-two-year-old, the *only* friend, who was brave enough to testify for Bill King. In the first trial, Gilbert Allen Cunningham said his former roommate King knew he dated a black woman, but that King only teased him about it and never made threatening comments, and never tried to persuade him to join a racist group.

Now Cunningham nervously tells this jury he saw Berry at the movie theater the day after the murder and that Berry asked him about the crime—if he knew whether the victim was black or white. Authorities say Berry denied ever speaking to Cunningham at his job that Sunday. Worse than that alleged lie is another. Berry has already told the jury he was with King at the car wash to clean up the chain and the truck. Cunningham, torn at his appearance, must think his testimony more important. "I saw Shawn at the car wash cleaning up his truck. He was alone."

Jurors look over at Berry and wonder if there are other versions to ponder. Then they are treated to the stern admonition Berry received from his probation officer, William Sparks. Ten months before the murder, he had warned Berry to stay away from Bill King. Others had also issued similar warnings—one came just two weeks before the crime.

Mary Verrett, one of the Byrd sisters, has become something of a family spokesperson. She is friendly, has an even-keel personality, and is quite popular among reporters for her willingness to grant interviews, even when she doesn't feel much like talking. Verrett is having a hard time concealing her impression that, even with the alleged discrepancies, Berry did well with his testimony. "He's a man that can't stand to see a person walking, but he can stand to see them dragged." When asked "Does Shawn Allen Berry deserve to die?" Verrett answers with a question of her own: "Did James Byrd, Jr., deserve to die?"

———

As closing arguments quickly wind down on Wednesday morning, November 17, Guy James Gray gets the final grit-sticking word: "Right now, you folks are the law in Jasper County." Gray does not talk long, but ends his statement with the proclamation that "Shawn Berry has got more blood on him than any one of the three." The ordeal, coupled with his sister's illness—she had surgery for a brain tumor during the trial—leaves Gray emotionally wiped out and physically exhausted. Prior to the third trial, I had a health threat of my own to contend with. Doctors found a lump on my right breast that they feared was cancer. Several mammograms, sonograms, and a painful breast compression took weeks to prove them wrong. I feel for his sister, and for Gray. He closes the state's evidentiary phase with one simple statement: "Under the facts and under the law, he is guilty of capital murder."

Finally, the end is near and Judge Golden puts Jasper one step from closure. "You may now retire to consider your verdict." Afterward, Gray talks to a herd of reporters. Many who have covered all three trials also share his pain: "That's all the fire I got in me."

Golden decides to give jurors until 9 P.M. to deliberate. If no verdict is reached by then, they will be sequestered, sleep on it, and start again in the morning.

Sand in the hourglass filters all the way through for George Coleman. After illness forced a juror off the panel, Coleman became the lone alternate. Now he is officially released and does not try to avoid the waiting media outside but eagerly talks to anyone who wants an interview. His comments do not bode well for the defendant—Coleman believes Berry lied from start to finish, and had he remained on the panel, his vote would be "guilty of capital murder."

Hours later, jurors want to know the definition of the word "secreting." Outside the DA's office, Brit Featherston, the government lawyer who looks about twelve, explains it to me fairly well. Featherston lets me hold a copy of the capital murder charge so I can study the document. "Secreting," he starts, "is more about concealment," which relates to the language contained in the kidnapping charge. In order to prove kidnapping, a prerequisite for a capital conviction, jurors must believe Gray's assessment that chaining Byrd's ankles fulfills the legal definition.

Pat Hardy drifts out into the hall from his office. He looks for and finds Featherston, then tells all the reporters an announcement is forthcoming. The stairs to the second floor are suddenly ripe with folks who speculate there may be a verdict. Hardy and I compare notes as we walk up together. We both urge the other to hang on, then go our separate ways.

After an all-day wait for the Byrd family that goes deep into the evening, the jury is tired. Hoping to hear that a decision has been reached, instead everyone is told, just before 10 P.M., to leave. Jurors need their rest and will resume deliberations very early in the morning. As all the noisy cliques walk out of the courtroom together, Shawn Berry's biological father, a man he has just met at this trial, musters up the courage to say a few words to the Byrd family.

At seven-thirty on Thursday morning, we get the first word on jurors: They are finished eating breakfast and immediately return to deliberating.

Two hours later, a note is sent out that a verdict has been reached. As bad as the reporters want to hear it, as do the families, spectators, prosecutors, and everyone involved, it cannot be read until Berry's attorney shows up. Lum Hawthorn finally arrives.

Judge Golden enters the courtroom to find out if both sides are ready. After more than ten hours of deliberations on guilt or innocence, both the prosecution and the defense answer in the affirmative. In the Standing Room Only courtroom, it is more crowded than usual—twenty-five Department of Public Safety officers are strategically positioned.

"Is there anyone present who cannot control their emotions?" the judge wants to know. Golden pauses and waits for someone to tell the truth. He tries again. "You need to leave if you cannot control your emotions when the verdict is read. I will not tolerate any outbursts." No one leaves. The jury is ushered in.

One by one, blank faces on seven women and five men do not surrender a single clue. There is not a worry line on a brow, a wayward pair of eyes, or anything else to suggest which fate they have chosen for the last "dragging" defendant.

As the verdict is delivered, there is a loud gasp at "Guilty of capital murder." It comes out almost in unison from both sides of the aisle. The audible sigh belongs to members from two families, one black, one white. They sigh for very different reasons. One feels vindication for a loved one; the other feels absolute dejection.

With his gavel, Judge Golden bangs a warning, but it is too late. Christie Marcontell collapses into a sea of tears, while the father of her baby shows no emotion. Berry may suffer a delayed reaction later, away from the media and spectators, but he appears to lock out any form of emotional display or self-pity because he is too busy. Berry has his hands full trying to comfort and quiet Marcontell. She cries loudly as more words emanate from the bench. Marcontell is so uncontrollable that even Judge Golden ignores his own threat to deal with anyone who cannot master their emotions. Berry puts his arm around the woman to whom he postpones marriage, then pushes their chairs closer together and tells her something private. Shawn Berry wears the appearance of bravery, but it is all show. His eyes are scared to death, scared of death. Judge Golden polls the jury. Berry looks, tries to listen, but still has his arm around Marcontell, who is near hysterics with sobs so loud I can barely hear.

Before Berry is escorted out of the courtroom, he and Marcontell hug a long time. Other Berry family members and friends come up to soothe and comfort the young woman, who just drops her head on the defense table and continues to wail.

In one hour, the penalty phase, already dubbed "High Noon in Jasper," will begin.

Things move at warp speed. The State of Texas rests without calling any witnesses to testify on punishment. Lum Hawthorn calls Louis Berry as the first witness for the defense. After his testimony in the evidentiary phase, Louis granted me an exclusive interview and admitted that he felt like he was the one on trial instead of his brother. Heartbreaking testimony begins with this man who is only eighteen months older than the one he now tries to save. Many of the same friends and family members who also testified before are back, all to plead for mercy. They sincerely beg for Berry's life. One of the jurors, and a couple of reporters, fight back tears.

Christie Marcontell is a drastically different witness this time. She talks through tears, mascara, and swollen eyelids. "I love Shawn very much. He loves that little boy more than anything in the world." The former beauty queen humbly tells the packed courtroom that she would give up everything she owns if the jury would simply vote life.

Hawthorn calls more than a dozen witnesses to petition the jury; they do not want Berry to die. Shawn Berry steps up as the final witness to ask for an alternative other than death.

Berry cries and asks the jury to spare his life. It is quite moving, until cross-examination, when Berry gets slapped with tough questions about his lack of remorse over the death of James Byrd, Jr. Before Brit Featherston finishes with Berry, he poses one of the most philosophical, chilling questions of the entire case: "Forty years from now, will a black man feel safe walking down Martin Luther King?"

At three-fifteen, the jury retires to think about the answer. If they vote life, Berry will be sixty-four years old before he is automatically eligible for parole.

A little more than an hour later, a Jasper County jury of his peers sentences Berry to life in prison. Berry and Marcontell embrace, cry tears of joy. Berry's family is all smiles, alight with joy over the confirmation that his life is worthy enough to save.

Guy James Gray makes his way to the bloated midsection of the courtroom and stands right in the aisle, full and redeemed. In a private moment before too many reporters walk up, I extend my hand to congratulate him, and Gray shocks me by pulling me close for a hearty hug. As one of the few journalists tapped to cover all three trials, Gray and I have formed an emotional bond, one that also connects me to Billy Rowles and Pat Hardy as well. As relieved as he is, I return the hug. A second later, we are joined by the familiar mob. Like a full man who unbuckles his belt after a feast, Gray delivers a minispeech: "Two death penalties and a capital conviction is pretty satisfying."

An old-fashioned heavy hum from above forces my head back, to look up at the eight ceiling fans that I had hoped that lonely day back in February in the empty Jasper County Courthouse would churn and cool the flame of racial bigotry. Justice blows cool, at least for now.

Byrd family members, still in their courtroom seats, cannot escape the reporters who surround them on the first two rows. "We can begin closure. It's all over," a female voice announces. Then Darrell Verrett: "My uncle can finally rest in peace and we can start the healing process." The most recognizable voice chimes in; it is Mary Verrett. "They have to live with their decision, one so many others did not want to make." Her sister, Clara Taylor, always opinionated, adds, "I still say he should receive the same penalty as the other two, but I do respect the decision of this jury." She is not the only one.

Across the room, Pat Hardy hands out interviews as reporters come up to congratulate him one by one. His position is clear. "I felt like the death penalty should have been evoked and I still do."

Wall-to-wall people, mostly reporters, stay in the courtroom to hang on for any nugget of spontaneous reaction or unfiltered heartfelt exchange. Judge Golden suddenly asks for quiet so the jury can reenter to read a prepared statement. The jury foreman, Gary Creel, stands uncertain and shaky. With tears in his eyes, Creel nervously starts, "Based on the facts and evidence presented in this case, we the jury have reached a unanimous decision after long hours of painful and prayerful deliberation." He continues, "We will not answer questions about this case now or at any time in the future. It is over." As they file out, one or two reporters have the audacity to yell ridiculous questions. Judge Golden makes a promise to deal with anyone who tries to contact a juror. Unlike his leniency and compassion for Christie Marcontell, I do not think Joe Bob plays with us.

Outside, the courthouse lawn is overrun with curious types, mostly residents who've just gotten off work or live in nearby towns like Buna, Woodville, Newton, and Kirbyville. They've heard about Berry's capital murder conviction and life sentence, and want to see him one more time. A few relish the idea that they are witnessing history in the making.

Berry is brought out a side door and poured into a waiting vehicle. Cheers and jeers greet him. Berry looks relieved, bewildered. He does not acknowledge the crowd or those who call to him. As the drama unfolds, I tell Dallas listeners, live, that Berry is getting into a car with Jasper County Sheriff Billy Rowles accompanied by voices he can never erase. One woman yells, "Shawn, we love you," while another counters, "At least you got better than Byrd."

Marcontell finds her way through the evening dusk to make a final statement to the media. She sighs, dropping her head to one side. "It's disappointing, but at least me and Montana are relieved we'll be driving to Huntsville for a visit, instead of an execution."

After the first conviction, Mary Verrett had told me back in February that the road to justice was "only one-third paved." I ask her what she would like to say about Berry, and four profound words take my breath away: "It is completed now."

Guy James Gray, a crowd favorite, stands in front of the slew of microphones. "Well, this is the last time." Reporters all laugh, and one yells back, "You know you're glad to be getting rid of us." I, for one, do not want to leave or just release these new people cast into my now different life. Gray is proud of the state's team; he thanks everyone who worked hard and had patience in the "hunt for justice."

As things slowly begin to loosen up, people drift back to their hotel rooms, some in amazement, others in gratitude. Many still have to work, to prepare for live shots on television stations across the country. After a brief interview with Hardy, two of my cell phones continue to ring. One caller, from CBS, wants me to do a debriefing that will include reports and a question-and-answer session, as well as a summary of the third trial.

I give radio listeners across the country a thirty-second snapshot of what I have just witnessed:

> The third dragging jury read a brief statement after sparing the life of Shawn Allen Berry. They will answer no questions now or ever about their decision. Earlier, the all-white jury deliberated for ten hours before returning with a capital murder conviction. When she heard it, Shawn Berry's fiancée became hysterical in the courtroom. Christie Marcontell had a much different reaction to Berry's life sentence. She and Berry embraced, something Marcontell says gave her strength. [Ten-second insert of Marcontell's comments on punishment.] Prosecutors say the jury had a tough job that nobody else wanted and they respect their decision. Joyce King, CBS News, Jasper, Texas.

Jeffrey Mullins, Jr., weighs a little more than 6 pounds and will never know the grandfather he is newly nicknamed for. To honor her father's memory, Renee Mullins sends word home from Hawaii that James Byrd, Jr.'s first grandson should rightfully wear the beloved family moniker "Son."

"Bittersweet" is the word Byrd family members use to describe the welcome news of a brand-new addition, one that arrives near the end of the third capital murder trial. On the courthouse lawn, they receive warm congratulations.

It was her pregnancy that kept Mullins away from the last two trials—doctors were concerned about all the stress. Renee is a lovely young woman, the oldest of the three Byrd children. Articulate and compassionate, I believe she will work long after the case ends to keep her dad's name and memory alive.

Byrd's only son, twenty-year-old Ross, did make an appearance at the first trial, as one of the angriest young men I have ever encountered. Between trials one and two, Ross graciously granted me a phone interview from his Fort Polk, Louisiana, army base. It is not therapeutic to talk about his father's gruesome murder. A soldier of few words, Ross told me he cannot even stand to be in the same room with any of the defendants.

The youngest child, sixteen-year-old Jamie, was in school during all three trials. And even if she hadn't been, I doubt protective family members would've allowed her to fully participate in the kind of media exposure and drama witnessed over the last few months. Before Jamie ever spoke with President Clinton, she told reporters that her best friend was white. She has no plans to change that.

While droves of drained reporters flee, glad to shake the dust of Jasper off their boots, Monique Nation (KRIV-TV), another reporter who covered all three trials, and I are among the tiny contingent of media representatives who will see it through to the end.

On Friday morning, November 19, 1999, Monique, a talented television star from the Fox station in Houston, and I drive to the Jasper City Cemetery for a special wreath-laying ceremony at the grave of James Byrd, Jr. In the morning dew, we stand on solemn, holy ground and wait for family members to arrive.

The integrated media assemblage consists of Monique, myself, Angel San Juan, Thomas Gandy, Bryson Hull, Willis Webb, Richard Stewart, and a couple of photographers. Though it is my first time at the grave site, Stewart, a sensitive reporter for the *Houston Chronicle*, has made many visits. So torn up about the vicious crime, Stewart comes to Byrd's grave every single day for months. I look over at him and smile as we all wait for the family to arrive. One by one, they show up with long faces but now less burdensome loads.

Family members reverently gather around Son's grayish-black marble headstone. One sister reads a poem; another fondly shares good wishes from around the world. As they talk, I am pressed into service. Darrell Verrett asks me to get some footage with a shiny silver Sony camcorder. I know at any moment my eyes will cloud and I won't be able to clearly see what I zoom in to capture. I do the best I can and watch the moving tribute on the small flip-out screen.

One of Mr. Byrd's nieces sings a favorite, "I Believe I Can Fly," and the other family members join in. They sing because he did, all the time. Then, James Byrd, Sr., whose voice I realize I never heard in any courtroom, says a few words. "Thank you for coming and for telling the world what happened to my son." I look around, out from behind the camera, to see reporters start to cry. It is therapeutic, the humble beginning of the healing process for a family that travels the long and winding journey to justice.

Another sister reads from two long ribbons that hang from a wreath of black and white carnations, merged, symbolically, I suppose, as a sign of unity. One ribbon is satiny white, the other black, and their words shimmer in gold glitter: JUSTICE FOR JAMES and FINALLY, REST IN PEACE.

Back at the Belle-Jim Hotel, where we've been camped out throughout our stay in Jasper, Monique and I sit down to breakfast. As we start, one of my cell phones rings; it is CBS. "Do you know anything about a special service the family is planning?" I swallow a mouthful. "Yes, it just ended." The familiar voice wants me to be on the next hourly newscast. There is not much left to say. Still, I find it hard to comprehend that the long pilgrimage really is over—for the family, and for me. But another more difficult one is just beginning as I attempt to sort out my own feelings on race.

Monique and I talk softly, stalling for more time. In the last year, she has quickly become one of my most beloved friends. We don't want to finish this breakfast because we are well aware it is the last time we will break bread for a while. She will return to her world in Houston, and my family in Dallas cannot wait to have me back. We push cold pancakes and brittle bacon around our plates, both in a strange mood. Someone comes in and snaps our picture together at the table. A few minutes later, the phone rings again: "Don't forget to call us to file that report."

As I gather my thoughts, I know I want to pay a fitting tribute to all that I've seen, a memorial in voice to the Byrd family and to justice. I also know that the network has only reserved about thirty seconds in the newscast for my summary, so I must choose words carefully to put listeners right at the headstone with me.

Slowly, I dial the desk in New York. They are ready to record my final network report on the "dragging," a word which no longer belongs to me. I cannot even use the phrase "dragging your feet" to procrastinating friends. It will, now and forever, always be attached to companion words—the "dragging" trials or a "dragging" death.

Relieved that this last set of public words will not be live, I am besieged by a plethora of emotions. Finding it hard to believe this is it, I take a deep breath, give the editor a count. "In three, two, one . . ." Then I file the following report:

It's justice. It's closure. Now that three white men have been punished for dragging a black man to death, the family of James

Byrd, Jr., gathered today to place a wreath at his grave. One sister read a poem. James Byrd, Sr., said farewell to his son, and a niece sang one of Byrd's favorite songs, 'I Believe I Can Fly.' As the others joined in, members of the media also cried. Shortly after, the family slowly and solemnly left the grave site, perhaps comforted by the knowledge that closure and justice finally means a soul is at rest. Joyce King, CBS News, Jasper, Texas.

CONCLUSION

In October 2000, the Texas Court of Criminal Appeals rejected John William King's argument that his trial did not prove he was guilty of murder, only that he is a racist. After nearly three years of a self-imposed media ban, King finally granted a death row interview to Mike Graczyk of the Associated Press. Mike has seen more executions than any journalist in the country and will probably be there when King is put to death. King told the AP correspondent that he wasn't present the night Byrd was murdered. He will fight until all appeals are exhausted.

Because King's case is on a "fast track," the path to an execution date is being paved with great speed, a reality that haunts his trial lawyer, Sonny Cribbs. "When you lose a death penalty case, even though it was bad, you don't get over it." He doesn't believe the State of Texas will gain anything by executing King, with the possible exception of making him a racist martyr to other white supremacists. In fact, Cribbs continues to get mail about his former client. A bold inmate in another state asked Cribbs to forward a letter to King. The man wanted King to write him back, solely to provide a description of what a thrill it must've been to kill a black.

Lawrence Russell Brewer, also on death row at the Terrell Unit, is now prisoner number 999327. Though the appeal process is also automatic for Brewer, it can take a number of years to complete. But the 1996 Antiterrorist Act, signed by President Clinton, has speeded up the process considerably. Each death row case, once taking an average of seven years, costs taxpayers more than $1 million dollars per prisoner. Federal law now allows inmates to present all writs at once, instead of over time, and also sets a one-year limit on an application for the habeas writ. No execution can be carried out as long as appeals remain active. Brewer's attorney Doug Barlow continues to fight for his client and vows to work until nothing else can be done.

Shawn Allen Berry is at the Ramsey Unit in Rosharon. He spends twenty-three hours a day in a 6-by-8-foot cell. As a Level One lifer, Berry is allowed out for one hour of recreation a day, alone. Berry has yet to be integrated into the general prison population and will remain in protective custody indefinitely for his own safety.

In 2001, the Ninth Texas Court of Appeals denied Berry's request for a new trial; his conviction was upheld after the court did not find alleged abuses pertaining to the jury and venue. Berry is not eligible for parole until he is sixty-four years old. Until then, he will celebrate all of his wedding anniversaries behind bars. Berry married Christie Marcontell by proxy.

After the third defendant was sentenced, Sheriff Billy Rowles ran for reelection and won. He still drives a white Ford F-250 truck. When pressed to remember the events of Sunday, June 7, 1998, he still gets tears in his eyes.

Pat Hardy continues in his position as assistant DA of Jasper County. When Hardy is not prosecuting the bad guys or deer hunting, he spends time competing and training kids in jujitsu. His tough-guy reputation precedes him wherever he goes in Texas.

His boss, Guy James Gray, is still the chief lawyer in Jasper County. The district attorney continues to weigh career options that could take him into private practice or to work for the government as a U.S. attorney. In July 2000, Gray and several members of the state's "dream team" were honored with prestigious awards from the United States Justice Department for their work on the case. Then–Attorney General Janet Reno presented the awards.

In 2001, as we stood close in Gray's office, he shared an intimidating message sent to him anonymously. It was a copy of an old photo—of five lynched black men. Gray has downed a lot of Jack Daniel's over this case; it nearly drove me to drink—so I understand.

As for the Byrd family, they continue to solicit funds for the James Byrd Jr. Foundation for Racial Healing, a project that allows them to go into elementary schools, distribute literature on tolerance, hand out scholarships, and fight racial violence. They are invited all over the country to speak at various events.

In 2001, a six-year battle to boost penalties for hate crimes was finally victorious. The James Byrd, Jr. Hate Crimes Bill was signed by Governor Rick Perry. Stella Byrd said it gives her something good to remember out of all the negativity associated with her son's murder.

The children of the victim also remain active on the national scene. Renee Mullins and Ross Byrd made appearances at the 2000 Democratic National Convention; Mullins spoke. Several Republicans blasted a newspaper ad she appeared in that urged voters to remember that then-Governor Bush had said no to previous hate-crime legislation named for her dad.

Mullins, along with the NAACP in Texas, has filed a wrongful-death lawsuit against King, Brewer, and Berry. The suit also names three unidentified individuals who "helped and encouraged" the three men, as well as the North Carolina–based Confederate Knights of America. Only the children are named in the lawsuit. Neither the parents nor the seven siblings of James Byrd, Jr., are participants.

In May 2001, I returned to my native Houston for the funeral of one of my dearest friends, Monique Nation. After the third trial, Monique fell ill. She was just thirty-six years old when she passed away, cancer having claimed one of the brightest lights that city has ever produced. Without Monique, I never would've made it through all three trials or had the courage to write this book. Her spirit is with me still.

Before the trials, I thought I wanted to be an anchor again, to prove that I still belonged at the white radio station that never appreciated me, no matter how many awards I won or how good I sounded. Now the anchor position doesn't hold the same meaning. Jasper has confirmed what I already knew—the professional is merged with the personal.

Pictures of Byrd and his last moments on earth still intermittently drift through my dreams. I was so affected by what I witnessed in Jasper, I decided to resign my position with CBS so I could spend this reflective period assessing the experience. I was also determined to find out more about the racism factories in Texas prisons and why my views on race in America were so dramatically altered by this case.

What I have learned is stark and sobering; we have much work to do in what is now the *second*-largest prison system in the country, after California. At the time of the crime, numerically, the Texas system was still the most populous. No matter what transpired behind prison walls before the crime, nothing can excuse the murder of James Byrd, Jr., or the tragic method utilized by the convicted killers. Nothing. But we must look at anything connected to the production of such hatred, whether it is the experience of men in prison or institutional racism from other sources. I know one thing for sure—erecting more prisons is not the answer, especially if a lot of these inmates are going to be released. That too is the law.

From all my interviews and conversations with prison officials, wardens, inmates, criminal consultants, and experts, one prevalent theme mentioned by all was respect. In prison, that appears to be what the larger fight is about. Everybody wants it; few understand what it will take to implement it in the system. One warden told me the whole system must be reconfigured. An ex-warden tended to agree, calling prison nothing more than "racial hotbeds" for breeding hatred.

Second, nonviolent offenders do not belong in prison units with inmates with a higher propensity for violence. They all too easily become immovable targets. It would not hurt Texas to modify its classification system for inmates, which helps officials determine where offenders will be housed and what kind of jobs they will be assigned. John William King, despite his defiant attitude and criminal mistakes, was one burglar who did not belong at the Beto Unit.

Another problem rests with the lack of diversity training for both guards and inmates. Having white rural Americans in charge of largely black and brown prison populations puts both corrections officers and inmates in extra danger. There is already a wedge of the unknown between them. As in the outside world, it gets larger and uglier when one, or both, do not respect the other's culture and background.

Texas is striving to make changes, slowly. Right after the dragging, state officials set aside an additional $350,000 dollars to study the problem of racist gangs and to educate the public on how they organize in prison. The murder of James Byrd, Jr., was credited with the decision to supply additional funding. It is a step in the right direction.

Thousands of corrections officers give 100 percent to their jobs. For the most part, they maintain law and order every day at the 110 prison units in Texas. But very few taxpayers have a clue about what they do. It is time to remove the veil of secrecy with effective dialogue between the public and prison officials. It has begun with a campaign to hire more minority officers and a push for higher wages and longer training. There is also a fairly new gang-renunciation program for inmates who want out of disruptive groups. It establishes an important line of communication and allows gang members to gradually ease themselves out of the racist gang mentality. A handful have graduated back into the free world.

With this case, I too have graduated to another level of understanding race in America, at least from the perspective of being born and raised in the South. It's a part of the world where not that many years ago white lawmen regularly instilled terror in the hearts of law-abiding black citizens, including members of my own family. It was a Sunday afternoon in East Texas when my mother, my aunt, and me took a drive that landed us in jail.

As was the custom of my family and neighbors, when we were on the road, we rarely drove alone, we memorized all the safe routes, and we were very careful to never have anything that might be misconstrued as contraband in the car. On our way back from Louisiana, my mother drove our car, while her sister and her children were in the car ahead. There was safety in numbers, or so we thought. A determined state trooper strategically nabbed both cars anyway, ticketing my aunt for impeding traffic and my mother for tailgating. Never mind that theirs were the only two cars on that lonely stretch of highway.

Angry with the white men who made my aunt cry and already pretending to be a reporter, I took out my little notepad and started to write down their names and other details. The sight of such a cocky black kid fiercely agitated one of the troopers. "What do you think you're doing?" he screamed. I fired right back: "We've got rights. You can't stop us for nothing."

When we were ordered to the nearest jail, I knew we were in trouble. I had heard the stories about how black people entered various Southern jails only to "disappear" and never be heard from again. After being denied our one phone call, deputies called the judge. When this person spoke to my mother, I studied her face. Whatever the judge said put the fear of God into my usually tough, thick-skinned mother. Two options emerged—spend that Sunday night in jail or come up with the cash to pay both fines.

A frantic search ensued. We looked in purses, luggage, even the cracks of car seats, to scrape enough money together for a police escort out of town. I won't forget how those white lawmen behaved, how funny they thought it was to frighten and detain two women and their young children.

Because of that experience and countless others, before Jasper, had I seen three people who looked and sounded like Guy James, Pat, and Billy, I would've crossed the street to avoid them and the stereotype I assumed they represented. But this case taught me what my own work on projects designed to promote racial tolerance had not. I was harboring my own insecurities about race and my own tendencies to stereotype. Recycling untruths simply made me more like the very people I avoided.

Equally important is what Jasper, Texas, taught me about justice. In the past, when black citizens found themselves enmeshed in a legal drama, I heard over and over, "No justice, *just us*." The universal declaration throughout American courtrooms usually referred to the number and the way in which black defendants were indicted, convicted, and incarcerated, and blacks altogether absented from the box of peers slated to determine their fate. Of the thirty-six jurists who decided the outcome of these three trials, only one was black. Predominantly white, and male, they had, apparently, taken to heart some of the lessons from tainted verdicts delivered in case after case during the Civil Rights era. One juror said it was important to get this one right.

When the last gavel sounded and justice was meted out, I truly felt that the boundaries of the New South extended into the court-rooms. And it isn't just in Jasper. From Louisiana to Florida, from the multiple trials for the man who killed Medgar Evers—Byron De La Beckwith—to the defendants in the 16th Street Baptist Church bombing, some of the very cases that broke this nation's collective heart are now being revisited.

The first time I stood on the road where a black man was chained to a pickup and dragged to his death, the car stereo played in the distance. Terrified, I had left the motor running in case I needed to make a hasty retreat. As I approached the car, John Lee Hooker's voice poured out loud and strong, "The blues is a healer. It can heal me, it can heal you too." There were a lot of nights in Jasper when I had the blues and longed for a good stiff drink to wash them down. Today another song has replaced the memory on Huff Creek Road.

At the last trial, Monique and I were given a cassette tape of James Byrd, Jr., singing. I had never even heard his voice. The lyrics, and a hate crimes bill in his name, are finally fulfilled and further inspire my own spiritual journey: "Precious Lord, take my hand, lead me on, let me stand. I am tired, I am weak, I am worn. Through the storm, through the night, lead me on, to the light."

No more blues for Byrd.

ACKNOWLEDGMENTS

A small circle of believers never faltered in their conviction that this book would be published. First and foremost, I thank the Creator from whence all blessings and challenges flow.

To my agent, Jane Gelfman, thank you for an endless supply of patience and direction. Dawn Davis, my faithful editor in the struggle, you were always there. Megan Hustad, your comments proved most insightful in the homestretch. Scott West, thanks for listening in the midnight hour. Dicia-Jane Howell for encouragement. Willis and Julie Webb, for answering a thousand questions. Mary Verrett, for unwavering support.

All my friends in Jasper, especially Carter, Billy, Guy James, and Pat, thanks a million. To my lawyer and Los Angeles confidant Michael Cohen, and my physician David Turner, thanks for advice, medicine, and support. To my second family at the Associated Press, for unmatched dedication and the copy machine, thanks, guys.

Love and kisses to the three men who constantly put up with long stints in pajamas and the reclusive behavior that kept me away from Little League games and high school football. Roderick Brion and Brandon Xavier, thank you for unconditional love. To your father, Rod, I have no words. You are truly the "go-to" guy in my corner. Someday, I hope to repay the favor.

Last, but not least, I thank my wonderful mother, Lida, who sold half my clothes to send me cash for supplies. Even when I wondered, she possessed blind faith this book would be finished.

Naturally, there are others who lent their time and expertise to this project. I thank everyone connected, great and small.

INDEX

Printed in the United States
by Baker & Taylor Publisher Services